T0334694

Cambridge Elements ≡

Elements in Language Teaching
edited by
Heath Rose
University of Oxford
Jim McKinley
University College London

EXTENSIVE READING

Jing Zhou
Zhejiang International Studies University

CAMBRIDGE
UNIVERSITY PRESS

Shaftesbury Road, Cambridge CB2 8EA, United Kingdom

One Liberty Plaza, 20th Floor, New York, NY 10006, USA

477 Williamstown Road, Port Melbourne, VIC 3207, Australia

314–321, 3rd Floor, Plot 3, Splendor Forum, Jasola District Centre,
New Delhi – 110025, India

103 Penang Road, #05–06/07, Visioncrest Commercial, Singapore 238467

Cambridge University Press is part of Cambridge University Press & Assessment,
a department of the University of Cambridge.

We share the University's mission to contribute to society through the pursuit of
education, learning and research at the highest international levels of excellence.

www.cambridge.org
Information on this title: www.cambridge.org/9781009474184

DOI: 10.1017/9781009474153

First published 2024

A catalogue record for this publication is available from the British Library

ISBN 978-1-009-47418-4 Hardback
ISBN 978-1-009-47417-7 Paperback
ISSN 2632-4415 (online)
ISSN 2632-4407 (print)

Extensive Reading

Elements in Language Teaching

DOI: 10.1017/9781009474153
First published online: December 2024

Jing Zhou
Zhejiang International Studies University
Author for correspondence: Jing Zhou, jingzhou@zisu.edu.cn

Abstract: This Element focuses on Extensive Reading (ER), a language learning and teaching approach that encourages language learners to read a large amount of interesting and level-appropriate reading materials. ER has been adopted across educational spectrums, including higher, secondary, and elementary levels, and implemented in diverse language contexts such as English, Chinese, Italian, Spanish, and French. The primary objective of this Element is to offer comprehensive insights into the theoretical foundations of ER, analyze its multifaceted benefits to language learning, address the challenges encountered in its implementation, and propose effective strategies drawn from research for these challenges. The Element concludes with an overview of the latest trends and developments in ER.

Keywords: extensive reading, definitions of ER, types of ER, benefits of ER, challenges and strategies of implementing ER, theories underlying ER, ER across languages, ER across contexts

ISBNs: 9781009474184 (HB), 9781009474177 (PB), 9781009474153 (OC)
ISSNs: 2632-4415 (online), 2632-4407 (print)

Contents

1 Introduction

This Element is intended as a helpful resource for language teachers, pre-service teachers, graduate students, and researchers interested in extensive reading (ER). My aim is to offer insights into how ER can be effectively implemented in various foreign or second language learning contexts. Drawing on a range of research, I hope to provide a concise yet comprehensive introduction to ER.

In Section 2, I introduce ER, beginning with its definitions and exploring theories underlying ER, such as Comprehensive Input Hypothesis, Lexical Efficiency Hypothesis, and Lexical Quality Hypothesis. This section also delves into the top ten principles of ER, concluding with an overview of different types of ER practices.

Section 3 highlights the linguistic and nonlinguistic benefits of ER. These include improvements in reading fluency, vocabulary, grammar, writing, and speaking, and positive impacts on reading attitude, motivation, reading habit, and flow experience. This section is based on a thorough review of ER literature, emphasizing its broad-reaching benefits.

Section 4 examines how ER has been implemented across languages. I first provide a description of the number of ER studies conducted across languages from 2018 to 2023, which shows that the majority of studies have been conducted in English as a foreign language (EFL) or English as a second language (ESL) context. Then I introduce ER studies in L2 Chinese, L2 Spanish, L2 German, L2 Japanese, L2 French, and L2 Italian. Acknowledging the limited studies in these areas, I do not distinguish between foreign and second language contexts, using "L2" to denote both. Section 5 focuses on the strategies and application of ER across contexts. Special attention is given to recent studies involving learners with advanced language proficiency, the unique challenges and opportunities in implementing ER in rural schools, and ER in English for academic purpose (EAP) contexts, and ER using online materials.

Section 6 addresses the challenges of implementing ER, considering the perspectives of students, teachers, institutions, and materials. Here, I share insights from current research and practical strategies developed by ER experts and practitioners. This includes approaches to curriculum design, material selection, teacher training, orientation, goal setting, and teacher guidance.

The Element concludes with a discussion on the future potential of ER, particularly its integration with other language teaching approaches and technology.

While this Element strives to be comprehensive, it is also a reflection of my ongoing learning journey in the field of ER. I hope it serves as a valuable starting point for those who share a passion for language teaching and learning.

2 What Is Extensive Reading?

2.1 Definition of ER

Reading extensively is how children become literate in their mother tongues. There is a saying in Chinese "读万卷书, 行万里路," which can be literally translated as "Read ten thousand books, travel ten thousand miles" to denote the importance of reading in Chinese culture. In their seminal book *Extensive Reading in the Second Language Classroom*, Day and Bamford (1998) systematically proposed ER as an approach to teaching and learning reading in a foreign or second language. ER involves reading large quantities of comprehensible texts. ER is also called *pleasure reading*, *free voluntary reading*, and *sustained silent reading* (Jeon & Day, 2016).

Day and Bamford (1998) defined extensive reading in a second language as "an approach to the teaching and learning of second language reading in which learners read large quantities of books and other materials that are well within their linguistic competence" (p. viii). Carrel and Carson's definition of ER is "extensive reading ... generally involves rapid reading of large quantities of material or longer readings (e.g., whole books) for general understanding, with the focus generally on the meaning of what is being read than on the language" (1997, pp. 49–50). Grabe and Stoller (2011) defined ER as "an approach to the teaching and learning of reading in which learners read large amounts of materials that are within their linguistic competence" (p. 286). Though the definitions by Day and Bamford (1998), Carrel and Carson (1997), and Grabe and Stoller (2011) differ slightly, what they share is first, ER involves reading a large amount of materials, and second, reading materials need to be comprehensible to readers. Those two features reflect the unique nature of ER and are reflected in two of the ER principles proposed by Day and Bamford (1998, 2002) (See section 2.3).

This approach completely differs from traditional approaches of teaching reading (such as intensive reading) in terms of "the quantity of reading, the difficulty level of the reading, the freedom students have to choose books, the degree of autonomy enjoyed by the students, and the motivation to continue reading" (Nakanishi, 2015, p. 9). Nation (2006) believed that through input at their level of proficiency, reading becomes a source of learning as well as a source of enjoyment.

After a discussion of its definition, the next section will focus on theories underlying ER.

2.2 Theories Underlying ER

In this section, I will discuss theories underlying ER. Those theories either provide theoretical justifications and rationales for the significance of ER or support the implementation of ER in language programs. One theory is Comprehensible Input Hypothesis proposed by Krashen, and the other three are Lexical Efficiency Hypothesis, Lexical Quality Hypothesis, and Lexical Constituency Model proposed by Perfetti and his colleagues. Since the latter three are closely related to each other, they will be discussed as one theory.

Comprehensible Hypothesis claims that we acquire language when we understand it, that is, when we get "comprehensible input" (Krashen, 1981). Comprehensible Hypothesis is a combination of two hypotheses, Input Hypothesis and Goodman/Smith Hypothesis, which states that reading is a natural process and learning is subconscious (Krashen, 2009). Krashen stated that Comprehensible Hypothesis holds for "first and second language acquisition, oral and written language, children, teenagers, and adults" (p. 57). There are a few key claims in this hypothesis. First, to facilitate language acquisition, the language input must be comprehensible. Krashen (1992) stated that "only comprehensible input is effective in increasing proficiency (p. 411). The more comprehensive input there is, the more language acquisition there will be. Second, language input needs to be interesting so that language learners or acquirers will pay attention to it. Third, a low affective filter or open attitude is needed. Krashen stated that activities that students reported to be least anxiety-provoking or non-anxiety-provoking, such as silent reading, seem to be very efficient in enhancing language acquisition. Lastly, the components of language such as vocabulary, grammar, spelling, writing, and so on are the results of getting comprehensible input. Numerous studies have shown that language was acquired merely by learners being very interested in reading (Krashen, 2009). For example, Krashen reviewed the Fiji Island study which showed that in-school free reading has a powerful effect on second language learners. The study divided a group of fourth- and fifth-grade students studying English as a second language into three groups. The first group used the audio-lingual method, an approach that emphasizes drill, repetition, and heavy grammar instruction. The second group did a free reading for the entire class (i.e., thirty minutes). In the third group, the teacher read the book to the students, students discuss the book, read it together, act out the story, and draw parts of the book. After two years, the free reading group and the shared reading group were superior to the traditional group in reading comprehension, vocabulary, and grammar tests. Another study that Krashen believed should be mentioned whenever free voluntary reading is discussed is the *Hooked on Books* project conducted by Daniel Fader and Elton McNeil (1968) (as cited in Krashen, 2009). They encouraged adolescent boys in a reform school to read newspapers, magazines, and paperback books. Students were also encouraged to share what they read with the class. After one year, the Scholastic Achievement Test scores showed that their reading comprehension scores increased by more than one entire grade level (1.3 years) and were twice as much as the scores of the students who did not read for pleasure. Thus, vocabulary, grammar, spelling, writing, and so on are the results of getting comprehensible input and can be learned incidentally through being immersed in reading.

Comprehensible Hypothesis is an important theory underlying ER since it highlights the importance of providing language learners comprehensible and interesting input and creating a low-anxiety environment, and as a result, different aspects of a foreign language will be acquired subconsciously.

Another theory underlying ER is related to word recognition. Lexical Efficiency Hypothesis, Lexical Quality Hypothesis, and Lexical Constituency Model, all attach great significance to the efficiency and quality of word recognition, an essential lower-level processing in reading. The hypotheses were proposed and tested by Perfetti and his colleagues (1985, 1992, 1999, 2007). Perfetti developed Lexical Efficiency Hypothesis in his book: *Reading Ability* (1985). This model assumes that for skilled readers, lower-level processing is relatively automatized. Word identification, the rapid retrieval of a word's phonology and meaning, is essential for comprehension. Lexical Efficiency Hypothesis was based on the notion that attention and working memory are limited resources. Efficient word recognition skills make fewer demands on attention and working memory and allow limited cognitive resources to be used for other higher-level comprehension processes, such as integrative processes, inferences, and syntactic repairs. According to Lexical Efficiency Hypothesis, each reader has a unique profile of verbal efficiency. The more efficient a reader's verbal efficiency is, the more cognitive resources can be allocated to higher-level processing. As a result, lexical efficiency, as the automatic and resource-cheap word-level processes, was assumed to support comprehension (Perfetti, 2007). Readers who have problems with higher-level comprehension skills may have inefficient word-identification skills (Grabe, 2009).

Lexical Efficiency Hypothesis is concerned with word reading fluency and decoding speed. It seems that by increasing the word recognition efficiency, the comprehension will be improved. However, an increase in word identification efficiency does not necessarily lead to better comprehension (Perfetti, 2007). Reading fast at the word level does not mean an accurate retrieval of word meaning and phonology that the reader needs in a given context. In order to have an accurate retrieval of word identification, a high-quality lexical representation is needed. Lexical quality refers to "the extent to which the readers' knowledge of a given word represents the word's form and meaning constituents and knowledge of word use that combines meaning with pragmatic features" (Perfetti, 2007, p. 359). Lexical quality is more about the depth of vocabulary knowledge, about whether the reader knows the form, the pronunciation, the meaning, and the usage of a word.

Lexical representation quality can be high or low. In order to distinguish high- and low-quality representations, Perfetti (2007) identified five features of lexical representation and three consequences of those features on the reading process. The representative features are the constituents of word knowledge: phonology, orthography, meaning, and grammar. Another feature, constituent binding, refers to the degree to which the four features, phonology, orthography, grammar, and meaning, are bound together to form a word's identity. The consequence of high lexical representation quality is stable and synchronous retrieval of a word from a mental lexicon, which is available for building comprehension. Low lexical representation quality, on the other hand, often leads to failure in retrieving the word identified from the mental lexicon, thus causing obstacles to comprehension.

Lexical representation quality to the accuracy and fluency of word identification. The higher quality the word representation is in a reader's mind, the faster and more accurately the word's identity will be retrieved. Also, the lexical representation quality may be related to different constituents of word knowledge. Some readers may have quality problems with the semantic constituent of a word; for most readers, the quality problem cuts across phonological, meaning, and orthographic constituents. Furthermore, readers differ in their word representations. Lexical representation quality is "graded across words for a given individual and across individuals for a given word" (Perfetti, 2007, p. 380). Finally, lexical representation quality originates from language experience. The more experience a reader has with a word, the better and more stable his lexical representation will be.

Both Lexical Efficiency Hypothesis and Lexical Quality Hypothesis were proposed based on research on alphabetical languages. Based on research on word reading in Chinese and alphabetical languages, Perfetti (2007) proposed the Lexical Constituency Model. The model assumes that a word representation consists of three interlocking constituents (or variables): orthography (OR), phonology (PH), and semantics (SE). Orthographic, phonological, and semantic constituents specify word identity. Thus, to identify a word involves the retrieval of a phonological form and meaning information from a graphic form. An absence of any one of the three constituents would result in an underspecified identity. Perfetti (2007) emphasized that the constituency framework is universal and not related to a specific writing system.

Lexical Efficiency Hypothesis, Lexical Quality Hypothesis, and Lexical Constituency Model provide strong theoretical support for extensive reading research and practice. ER provides meaningful contexts for the acquisition of words. The more learners read, the faster they recognize words. Numerous empirical studies have also provided evidence for the learning of different aspects of vocabulary knowledge (e.g., spelling, meaning, and usage) through reading. A large sight vocabulary size enables the efficient and automatic recognition of words. As a result, this efficient, automatic, and high-quality lower-level processing will enable more cognitive recourses to be allocated to higher-level processing.

Nassaji (2014) stated that there are three perspectives in the past few decades regarding both L1 and L2 reading research: bottom-up, top-down, and interactive views of reading (p. 2). The bottom-up approach views reading as "consisting of a series of successive stages, starting with a visual analysis of letters and sounds, then combining them to construct phrases and sentences, and finally building a semantic representation of the text" (Nassaji, 2014, p. 2). Top-down approach views reading as primarily a "reader-driven activity" (p. 2) and that reading comprehension mainly relies on readers' conceptual and background knowledge. Readers verify top-down hypotheses by using strategies such as predicting and guessing (e.g., Goodman, 2014). The interactive view perceives reading as composed of several component skills that interact with each other. Though the three perspectives have been proposed and tested in reading research, a feature of the most current view of L2 reading, as Nassaji (2014) has pointed out, is the importance of lower-level processes.

To conclude, efficient reading comprehension in a second language (L2) hinges on the reader's proficiency in lower-level processes. These foundational skills are essential for allocating cognitive resources effectively to more advanced levels of comprehension. As evidenced in Nassaji's (2014) systematic review, even advanced L2 readers rely significantly on these lower-level processes. An important takeaway from Comprehensible Hypothesis, Lexical

Efficiency Hypothesis, Lexical Quality Hypothesis, Lexical Constituency Model, and the current L2 reading research is the need for L2 reading instruction to focus on developing these essential lower-level skills. In this context, extensive reading emerges as a pivotal method of teaching and learning reading. It improves L2 reading comprehension and language proficiency in general through facilitating the enhancement of these crucial lower-level processes.

Points to Ponder
- What do you think is the relationship between vocabulary knowledge and reading proficiency?
- Do you agree with Comprehensible Input Hypothesis? Why or why not?

2.3 ER Principles

Since ER is an approach to teaching and learning L2 reading, language teachers need to know how to implement ER in their language classrooms. Day and Bamford (2002, pp. 137–140) proposed the ten principles of implementing ER.

1. The reading material is easy.
Easy here means that reading materials must be "well within" the learners' reading competence in the foreign language (Day & Bamford, 2002, p. 137). This principle may particularly apply to learners with low language proficiency (e.g., Nishizawa et al., 2018). For beginning-level learners, more than one or two unknown words will make the text too difficult for overall understanding. For intermediate-level learners, no more than five difficult words per page can be used. Day and Bamford (2002) believed that this principle separates ER from other approaches, such as intensive reading. By reading materials that are easy and enjoyable and reflect their language ability, students will enjoy reading, want to read more, and ladder up as their reading skills and language proficiency improve. It also needs to be noted that to achieve optimal reading experience, reading materials should match learners' reading abilities. When learners' reading abilities improve, they should be suggested to read higher-level books that match their language proficiency.

2. There must be a wide variety of reading material on a large range of topics.
There needs to be a variety of reading materials of different genres and with different topics for learners to choose from. Varied reading materials enabled

students to read for different purposes (e.g., entertainment, information, general understanding) and in different ways (e.g., careful reading; skimming) (Day & Bamford, 2002). For example, advanced German readers in Arnold (2009) read a variety of online materials of diverse genres (e.g., news, blogs, fiction) and topics (e.g., travel, cultures, entertainment, media, sports, education, professional life, society, hobbies, science, nature, commentary, and so on).

3. Students choose what they want to read.

Learners have the freedom to choose what they want to read and also the freedom to stop reading if the material is not interesting, too easy, or too difficult. ER research so far has established the importance of this principle (e.g., Fongpaiboon, 2017). L2 readers in general prefer to read materials selected by themselves and enjoy the autonomy of book selection.

4. Learners read as much as possible.

Day and Bamford (2002) claimed that this principle is the "extensive" of extensive reading (p. 138). The most crucial element in learning to read is the amount of time spent actually reading. Day and Bamford (2002) suggested one book a week be a realistic target for learners of all proficiency levels. With online reading platforms like Xreading.com, some ER programs also set a number of words read per week as a reading target, for example, 10,000 words for intermediate readers and 12,000–13,000 words per week for advanced level in an EAP program in Zhou and Day (2021). Research has revealed the significance of setting clear reading goals in enhancing extrinsic reading motivation (see Section 6.2.5).

5. The purpose of reading is usually related to pleasure, information, and general understanding.

In an ER program, learners are encouraged to read for the same purposes as the general population of first-language readers (Day & Bamford, 2002), that is, for information, for enjoyment, and for general understanding. It is different from intensive reading where the purpose of reading is usually related to linguistic study and students need to complete many language or comprehension-related exercises. The objective of ER is to develop enthusiastic second language (L2) readers who find joy in reading.

6. Reading is its own reward.

Extensive reading is not usually followed by comprehension questions since reading in ER is for the sake of reading. However, teachers may ask students to complete follow-up activities based on their reading. Researchers have compiled lists of ER activities (e.g., Bamford & Day, 2004; Leather & Uden, 2021). Students may be asked to write a different ending for the story, letters to the main characters, book reports, and so on. The reasons for the reading activities are to check students' comprehension, to keep track of students' reading records, and to create a community of readers, among others. Online ER websites like Xreading.com or Mreader also have quizzes that students can complete after reading. Ponndy Reader, an online Chinese language learning platform, also has grammar and vocabulary exercises that students can complete.

7. Reading speed is usually faster rather than slower.
When learners read reading material that is well within their language proficiency and is of interest, their reading speed is usually faster than slower. Learners are discouraged from using dictionaries to look up unknown words because this will interrupt the reading process. As learners read more and more, their abilities to guess the meaning of unknown words from contexts improve. Learners may feel comfortable with a certain level of ambiguity. Moreover, reading speed is fast because learners have a large size of sight vocabulary, which means that they can recognize words efficiently and automatically (Day, 2013).

8. Reading is individual and silent.
ER allows students to discover that reading is a personal interaction with the text. Students can read silently in class when a portion of class time is set aside for ER or read outside of the classroom at home, in the library, on a sofa, or in a cozy bed. Though reading itself is silent and individual, after reading discussion or sharing can be pair, group, whole class, or whole society activities. For example, *Bibliobattles* is a social book review game that combines silent reading with public sharing of books (Maclauchlan, 2018) and has been used in some ER programs.

9. Teachers orient and guide their students.
As an approach to teaching reading, ER is very different from how reading has traditionally been taught in language classrooms in many contexts. Thus, the teachers need to give orientation to the students at the beginning of an ER program. Teachers can explain the nature of ER, its main principles, benefits of ER, and assessment. Teachers can instruct students on the reading materials, either a school or classroom library or an online platform, and how to select appropriate books to read. Day and Bamford (2002) claimed that guidance throughout the ER program is needed. Teachers can keep track of how much students have read, their reactions to the materials, and their

feelings in the process. One thing very important for teachers to do is to encourage students to read at progressively higher levels of difficulty as their reading ability and language ability improve.

10. The teacher is a role model of a reader.

ER teachers are themselves readers. ER teachers can read what students read. This way teachers can discuss the books with students, answer their questions, and recommend books to each other. Tabata-Sandom (2023) read books on Xreading.com with her participants and recommended books to them in Newsletters regularly sent out to the participants.

There are reasons why certain principles may not be adhered to. For instance, some learners may prefer more challenging materials, especially advanced learners (see Arnold, 2009) or those with stronger motivation. This means that principle #1 might not be suitable for all types of learners. Moreover, as one reviewer highlighted, teachers often cannot serve as role models for reading because (1) much of the reading is done outside the classroom, and (2) not all teachers are avid readers themselves. This situation somewhat contravenes the final principle.

Since Day and Bamford proposed the ten principles in 2002 as a framework for the implementation of ER, these guidelines have been the subject of extensive discussion, evaluation, and research among both language educators and scholars. Macalister (2015, p. 122) categorized the ten principles into four types: *the nature of reading, the nature of reading material, what the teachers do*, and *what the students do* (Table 1).

Macalister (2015) claimed that in some learning contexts, learner choice (principle #3) and having a wide variety of materials available for learners to choose from (principle #2) may not always be possible. In addition, sometimes teachers may decide that reading is not for its own sake and for pleasure (principle #6), but as a springboard for another language learning activity (Macalister, 2015). Similarly, Ng et al. (2019) suggested that Principle #6 could be replaced with "Reading will need to be monitored and assessed" (p. 173). Macalister proposed top seven ER principles and deleted principles #2, #3, and #6 from the list. Learning contexts, students' needs, and logistic issues all influence how ER will be conducted. It is essential to take those factors into consideration when designing and implementing ER programs.

ER practitioners adhere to the ten ER principles in various ways, ranging from strict to loose application and from full to partial implementation. The ten principles have played a significant role in the development of ER and many studies employed the ten principles as a framework for the establishment of ER

Table 1 Categorizing the top ten principles for extensive reading (adapted from Macalister, 2015).

The nature of reading

5. The purpose is usually related to pleasure, information, and general understanding
6. Reading is its own reward
7. Reading speed is usually faster rather than slower
8. Reading is individual and silent

The nature of the reading material

1. The reading material is easy
2. A variety of reading material on a wide range of topics must be available

What the teachers do

9. Teachers orient and guide their students
10. The teacher is a role model of a reader

What the learners do

3. Learners choose what they want to read
4. Learners read as much as possible

programs or implementation of ER practices (e.g., Arnold, 2009; Bui & Macalister, 2021).

Day (2015) reexamined how the ten ER principles were used in forty-four ER programs. The results (see Table 2) showed that principle #3 *Learners choose what they want to read* was the most often used principle (thirty-eight programs). Freedom of book choice was perceived as a pleasure experience and a strong motivating factor in ER studies (Arai, 2022).

Three other principles were also widely used:

Principle #4 Learners read as much as possible (thirty-six programs)
Principle #2 A variety of reading material on a wide range of topics is available (thirty-five programs)
Principle #1 The reading material is easy (thirty-four programs).

Another frequently used principle was *principle #8 Reading is individual and silent (thirty-one programs).*

To conclude, language teachers are encouraged to select which principles to apply, taking into account the specific contexts of their teaching environments.

Table 2 The practice of ten ER principles in forty-four ER programs (adapted from Day, 2015).

Principles	Times used
#3. Learners choose what they want to read.	38
#4. Learners read as much as possible.	36
#2. A variety of reading material on a wide range of topics is available.	35
#1. The reading material is easy.	34
#8. Reading is individual and silent.	31
#5. The purpose of reading is usually related to pleasure, information, and understanding.	28
#6. Reading is its own reward.	23
#7. Reading speed is usually faster rather than slower.	20
#9. Teachers orient and guide their students.	18
#10. The teacher is a role model of a reader.	8

Points to Ponder
- Which of the ten ER principles do you think are the most important for a successful ER program?
- Can you think of other principles that can guide an ER program?

2.4 Types of ER

There might be no single type of ER. Based on whether ER programs fully or partially followed the ten ER principles, Day (2015) classified ER into four types: *pure ER*, *modified ER*, *ER light*, and *fringe ER*. *Pure ER* uses all the ten ER principles. *Modified ER*, as Day (2015) put it, uses many ER principles. *ER light* uses some of ER principles. The last one, *fringe ER*, uses none of the ten principles, thus it is "ER in name only" (p. 296).

Given the various types of ER and different practices of ER, Day (2015) suggested that ER principles can be used based on the nature of ER programs. An examination of ER literature reveals that language teachers use a variety of labels to describe their ER programs. The following are some examples.

Replacement ER

The time usually spent on other classroom activities is replaced by ER (Robb & Kano, 2013). For example, the control group in Aka (2019) studied grammar for two hours while the ER group read extensively in class.

Additive ER

Additive ER occurs outside of class hours and thus provides additional language contact time for learners (Robb & Kano, 2013). Robb and Kano (2013) implemented additive ER among 2,586 nonmajor first-year EFL college students at Kyoto Sangyo University in Japan. All students taking one English class were required to read five graded readers outside of class time and if they took more than one English class, the number of books was doubled or tripled. Students would lose five points from their final grade if the ER requirement was not completed. Five points were added to their grade if they doubled the requirement. The additive ER only required teachers to distribute a handout that explained ER in Japanese, the reading requirement, how to check out books, and how to take quizzes using MoodleReader (i.e., MReader). The reading results were distributed to each teacher at the end of each semester. MoodleReader allowed students to take short, timed quizzes on the books they read. After comparing the reading and listening test scores, it was revealed that students who did additive ER performed significantly better compared to students who did not participate in additive ER one year ago. The authors believed that the implementation of addictive ER at Kyoto Sangyo University has been successful because of a number of reasons: (a) The school administration was able to require the implementation of ER among the entire nonmajor English language course curriculum; (b) MoodleReader, the quiz platform, held students accountable for their reading and relieved teachers from record keeping; and (c) the university library was supportive and purchased the required number and variety of graded readers.

Supervised ER

Supervised ER does not necessarily have to take part in a school or university. It is a type of ER where readers do ER while being supervised or guided by ER mentors. For example, Ro (2013) described his role as a mentor who "sat close by reading [his] own English books, and responded to her [Lisa, a Korean EFL learner] questions about the storyline, word or phrase meanings, and grammatical structures" (p. 218). In Tabata-Sandom's (2023) study, she recruited eleven ER participants via Facebook groups and a local book club to participate in an online ER project. Mitsue sent weekly newsletters to the participants, recommending books and reporting the participants' reading progress. She also sent out individually tailored encouragement to the participants. Her role is similar to that of Ro. The main difference is that she was a mentor for a group of advanced readers while Ro was mentoring one learner.

Independent ER (noninstructed)

This ER practice involves an individual or individuals engaging in ER with no supervision. Leung (2002) reported she had engaged in ER in order to learn Japanese. She borrowed books from friends and a local library. In nine weeks, she read 32 books or about 1,260 pages. Any L2 learner who is motivated to read can adopt this approach. Learners can also seek guidance or help while doing independent ER. For example, Leung (2002) asked for help from her professors regarding book choice and met a Japanese friend every week to ask questions about the Japanese language. Another example of independent ER was reported by Krulatz and Duggan (2018). The two researchers were also the participants. They learned Norwegian through extensive reading while teaching English at a local institution.

Blended Extensive and Intensive Reading

This approach is a combination of intensive reading and extensive reading. The intensive reading part focuses on the teaching of reading strategies while the extensive reading part fosters reading fluency.

The diverse implementations of ER demonstrate that it is a flexible approach, adaptable to a wide range of learning contexts and individual student needs. This flexibility allows language teachers to choose from various ER types, depending on the specific goals and constraints of their educational setting. Whether it's replacing traditional classroom activities, adding extra reading outside class hours, providing supervised reading sessions, encouraging independent reading, or blending intensive and extensive reading methods, each variation of ER can be customized to suit the unique linguistic and developmental needs of language learners. This adaptability ensures that ER remains an effective and responsive approach in the evolving landscape of L2 reading.

> **Points to Ponder**
> 1. Reflecting on the different types of ER described, which type do you think would be most effective in your current or future teaching context, and why?
> 2. Which ER types do you believe would be most beneficial for beginners versus advanced learners, and why?

3 The Benefits of ER

Numerous studies have been conducted to examine the effects of ER as compared to other approaches to teaching reading (e.g., Chan, 2020; Jeon & Day, 2016; Nakanishi, 2015; Nation & Waring, 2019). Before delving into the effects of ER on specific aspects of language learning such as reading speed, vocabulary knowledge, grammar knowledge, and writing abilities, I would like to provide a general introduction to its effects on language learning based on the results of a few meta-analyses.

After reviewing 34 studies with a total sample size of 3,942 participants, Nakanishi's (2015) study revealed that students who received ER instruction outperformed students who did not by a medium effect size for both experimental-control group contrasts ($d = 0.46$) and pre-post contrasts ($d = 0.71$). That is to say, participants with extensive reading instruction yielded better *reading proficiency outcomes* (i.e., reading speed, reading comprehension, vocabulary, grammar and other combined) than ones with other methods of instruction.

Gathering 71 unique samples from 49 studies and involving a total of 5,919 participants, Jeon and Day's (2016) meta-analysis revealed a small to medium effect for experimental-control group contrasts as well ($d = 0.57$). This, as Jeon and Day claimed, indicates "the superiority of the ER group over the intensive or traditional reading group" (p. 253). Similarly, the overall effectiveness of ER in pre-post groups is small to medium ($d = 0.79$). Please note that the two studies used different guidelines for determining the size of effects. Nakanishi (2015) adopted Cohen's (1988) guidelines (small $d \leq 0.2$, medium $0.2 < d < 0.8$, large $d \geq 0.8$) while Jeon and Day (2016) used Plonsky and Oswald's benchmark (2014) (group contrast: small $d = 0.4$, medium $d = 0.7$, large $d = 1.0$; pre-post contrast: small $d = 0.6$, medium $d = 1.0$; large $d = 1.4$).

The two meta-analyses conducted moderator analysis. First, as for learners' age. Nakanishi (2015) found that ER might be more beneficial for older participants (e.g., $d = 0.61$ for high school students, $d = 1.12$ for university students, and $d = 1.48$ for adults in pre-post comparison). In Jeon and Day's study, the highest mean effect size was also found in the adults group ($d = 0.70$), which refers to college students and above. Overall, it seems that ER might be more beneficial for later learners. Nakanishi (2015) explained that this might be related to the maturity of learners. As age increases, learners may understand the content better, which could motivate them to read more. In both meta-analyses, the number of studies with children and adolescent learners as participants were less compared to those with college students and above. Thus both Nakanishi (2015) and Jeon and Day (2016) called for caution in interpreting the results and more studies conducted with young learners.

As for the length of ER program treatment, Nakanishi (2015) found that one-year instruction (i.e., from more than six months to one year) produced effect sizes of $d = 0.52$ and $d = 0.74$. for group and pre-post contrasts, respectively. The effect sizes of other lengths of ER instruction, such as one semester (less than three months) and two semesters (from three to six months), were smaller. However, Jeon and Day (2016) did not find a significant difference among different lengths of ER programs in group comparisons. It needs to be noted that in Nakanishi (2015), there were no ER studies that lasted over one year and in Jeon and Day (2016), only four studies had ER instruction lasted over one year. This calls for research on more longitudinal ER studies. Actually, some longitudinal ER studies have been conducted in recent years, such as for one year (Aka, 2019; Mermelstein, 2015; Puripunyavanich, 2022; Tabata-Sandom, 2023) and 2.5 years (e.g., Nishino, 2007).

Among reading rate, reading comprehension, and vocabulary, reading rate showed a notably higher effect size ($d = 0.83$) than reading comprehension ($d = 0.54$) or vocabulary ($d = 0.47$) in Jeon and Day (2016). With regard to group contrasts in Nakanishi (2015), effect sizes of $d = 0.98$ for reading speed and $d = 0.63$ for reading comprehension were identified. The confidence interval of the effect size of vocabulary included 0. Turning to pre-post contrasts, a large effect for vocabulary ($d = 1.25$) and a large effect for reading comprehension ($d = 0.72$) were obtained. The confidence intervals of the effect size of reading speed included 0. Although there are no consistent results regarding which linguistic aspect ER exerted the most influence on, it can be stated that ER plays an important role in reading speed, vocabulary knowledge, and overall reading comprehension.

Language teachers have reported observing various benefits associated with the use of ER in language teaching. For example, Chang and Renandya (2017) collected data on the main reasons for implementing ER from 119 teachers in Asian contexts. Almost 82.4% of the teachers considered ER important for enhancing learners' overall language proficiency, 68.9% of them believed that ER was beneficial in enhancing reading competence, and 41.2% of them considered ER enjoyable. Teachers also listed other reasons for implementing ER, such as to enhance students' intrinsic motivation for learning, to gain confidence, to set their habit of reading, to foster lifelong reading habits, to ignite a joy for reading, to learn about other cultures, and so on.

The following sections will focus on the benefits of ER on reading fluency, vocabulary, grammar, writing, listening, speaking, flow experience, reading attitude, reading motivation, and reading habit.

3.1 Reading Fluency

Reading fluency is a critical concept in both L1 and L2 reading research. According to Kuperman et al. (2023), "high reading proficiency is not only about comprehending the text being read but also doing it fluently" (p. 8).

Fluency is viewed as an essential step in the comprehension of reading texts. Fluent reading involves *automaticity*. Reading fluency refers to the ability to *automatically recognize* an increasing number of words and phrases (Day, 2013; Taguchi et al., 2004). Fluent reading also involves *accuracy*. When people read fluently, the automatic word recognition is always accurate (Day, 2013). Words that readers recognize quickly, rapidly, and accurately, are called *sight vocabulary*. Fluent readers have *effective* and *efficient* word recognition skills and thus usually have a large sight vocabulary. When learners encounter the same words many times, these words may enter their sight vocabulary (Day & Bamford, 1998). Day (2013) viewed sight vocabulary as one point on the continuum of reading vocabulary. On one end of the continuum are words that readers don't know. In the middle of the continuum are words that are in the readers' general vocabulary. General vocabulary requires readers to pause for one or two seconds to recall their meaning (Day, 2013). When learners read a lot, they encounter words that are part of their general vocabulary. When readers come across the same words over and over again, the general vocabulary may enter into readers' sight vocabulary. This is how extensive reading helps readers become fluent readers.

Thus, it is critical that learners have opportunities to keep seeing the words that they have seen before. Iwahori (2008) investigated how ER improved the reading speed among thirty-three Japanese high school EFL learners. The students were asked to read twenty-eight books (graded readers and comic books) over seven weeks. Students' reading rate was assessed at the beginning and end of the ER treatment through one-minute reading probe method (i.e., word per minute [WPM]). The results of a paired t-test revealed that there was a significant reading rate increase, from 84.18 WPM (pre-test) to 112.82 (post-test). The increase of 28.64 WPM indicated that reading rates were shown to increase by about 30 percent in the ER treatment period. Similarly, after reading on Xreading.com for one year, the 11 advanced, post-tertiary L2 learners in Tabata-Sandom (2023) increased their reading rate from 123.8 WPM to 153.2 WPM, an increase rate of 23.6 percent. In another study, seventeen English learners from a university in Vietnam read on an online extensive reading website for ten weeks (Bui & Macalister, 2021). The average number of words read by the participants in 10 weeks is 23,409 words. Bui and Macalister (2021) used four methods to calculate the reading rate increase and the most conservative method showed the participants' reading speed on average increased thirty-six WPM, which is approximately an increase of 23%. Almost 70% of the participants (twelve out of seventeen) agreed that the online ER program helped them read more fluently.

While investigating reading fluency, ER has also been compared or combined with other approaches. Bell (2001) investigated extensive reading versus intensive reading with young adult EFL learners in Yemen and compared the reading rate changes of the two groups. The intensive reading group's reading rate increased from 78.45 WPM to 92.54 WPM, while the ER group increased from 68.10 WPM to 127.53 WPM. In a similar vein, after reading extensively for one semester, 34 first-year Japanese EFL students at a private, four-year nursing college in Japan improved their reading speed from 110.59 WPM to 131.33 WPM (Huffman, 2014), which was similar to that achieved by the group that read simplified texts (16.85 WPM) in Beglar et al. (2012). Research has also shown that the participants who read the most made the greatest reading rate gains (Beglar & Hunt, 2014).

The average silent reading rate for adults in English is 238 WPM for nonfiction and 260 WPM for fiction (Brysbaert, 2019), and the reading rate of second or foreign language learners is much slower. Considering the role that reading fluency plays in reading comprehension, L2 learners should be provided with abundant opportunities to read (e.g., Beglar & Hunt, 2014). Learners who read level-appropriate and intriguing materials read faster, comprehend more, enjoy more, and want to read more, entering the so-called "virtuous circle of the good reader" (Nuttall, 1996).

Points to Ponder
- Provide specific examples to illustrate how fluency, or a lack thereof, has impacted comprehension in real reading situations based on your experience learning or teaching an L2.
- Could you think of some strategies to train reading fluency?

3.2 Vocabulary

The significance of vocabulary in learning a foreign language cannot be overestimated. Research has shown that incidental vocabulary learning through reading occurs for both L1 and L2 learners. ER studies have suggested that graded readers can be an important source of vocabulary learning for L2 learners (e.g., Bourtorwick et al., 2019; Daskalovska, 2018; Iwata, 2022; Jeon & Day, 2016; Liu & Zhang, 2018; McQuillan, 2020; Nakanishi, 2015; Pigada & Schmitt, 2006; Tabata-Sandom, 2023). A meta-analysis of the effects of ER on English vocabulary learning showed that ER had a large effect ($d = 1.32$) for experimental versus control group comparison and a huge effect ($d = 3.26$) for pre-post comparison (Liu & Zhang, 2018). In another meta-analysis by Nakanishi (2015), a large effect of ER on vocabulary ($d = 1.25$) was obtained for pre-post comparison. In Jeon and Day (2016), ER had a medium effect ($d = 0.47$) on vocabulary.

Considering the large effect of reading on vocabulary learning, researchers such as Krashen (2004) advocated free voluntary reading as the main route for acquiring new vocabulary. When students do a lot of reading, they have multiple meaningful encounters over time with words. Their vocabulary size tends to increase, and they also learn new meanings or usages of words they already knew. Compared with the direct instruction of vocabulary, the incidental learning of vocabulary through reading has proven to be more efficient (e.g., McQuillan, 2019). Pigada and Schmitt (2006) listed a few reasons why it is very "attractive" to develop vocabulary knowledge through extensive reading (p. 2). First, ER is considered a pedagogically efficient approach because vocabulary learning and reading occur at the same time. Second, ER provides learners with the opportunity to meet words in their contexts of use. Third, learning vocabulary through ER can be pleasant and motivating, which, as a result, may facilitate learner autonomy.

As for factors affecting the vocabulary gains through ER, frequency of encounters (e.g., Pigada and Schmitt, 2006) and learners' language proficiency (Park et al., 2018) have been demonstrated to play a role. The more a word is encountered, the higher the chance it is to be acquired. Previous studies have also endeavored to determine how many times a word needs to be encountered before learning occurs. As Nakanishi (2015) argued, "One key to successful foreign language vocabulary acquisition is the opportunity to meet the same lexis repeatedly in communicative contexts; extensive reading can be of enormous assistance in this endeavor." (p. 10). Of course, studies have also shown that some words are just more difficult to acquire. For example, *G*, a L2 French learner in Pigada and Schmitt (2006) had difficulty learning words such as *entendre* ("to hear") and *le radeau* ("raft") incidentally even after 20+ encounters.

Numerous empirical studies have been carried out to demonstrate the impact of ER on vocabulary acquisition. With sixty-one Taiwanese EFL learners as participants, Webb and Chang's (2015) study found that vocabulary gains were 44.06% after reading ten graded readers and 36.66% after three months. Serrano (2023) investigated English science vocabulary learning through reading nonfiction graded readers of scientific content in a one academic year long ER program. The participants were ninety-six Spanish primary school learners of English. The study showed that extensive reading and reading while listening produced an average immediate and long-term relative gain of 50.43% and 47.76% in vocabulary in Term 1. Tabata-Sandom (2023) showed that after reading online for one year, the average vocabulary size (measured by VocabularySize.com) of eleven advanced L2 learners increased from 7,081 to 8,481 word families, which is a 19.8 percent gain rate.

In some ER studies, vocabulary knowledge is equivalent to word meaning knowledge. However, it should be noted that there are different aspects of vocabulary knowledge. According to Nation (2001), there are twenty-six aspects of vocabulary knowledge categorized into three types: form, meaning, and use. Thus, scholars in the field suggested that more attention should be paid to other aspects of vocabulary knowledge and measure partial learning of the knowledge. For example, Pigada and Schmitt (2006) examined how G, a 27-year-old L2 French learner, acquired 133 words (70 nouns and 63 verbs) while reading extensively. The study tested the learning of spelling, meaning, and use of 133 target words through a comparison of a pre-post vocabulary test. The graded readers G read were from the "Lectures CLE *en Francais facile*" collection (Level 1). The vocabulary lists of those readers ranged from 400 to 700 words. G read four graded readers in one month, which was 228 pages in total with approximately 30,000 words. G had no other French exposure apart from the graded readers. The results showed that there was a relatively strong enhancement in the spelling of the target words. G spelled 98 out of 266 (36.8 percent) words correctly in the pre-test. However, G spelled 159 out of 266 (59.8) words correctly in the post-test. This finding suggests that ER can be very beneficial for the spelling of French words, which are considered difficult to learn. This accords with Day and Swan's claim of the "causal relationship" between foreign language reading and spelling (1998, p. 1). Next, the word meaning knowledge increased from 22 points out of 266 (8.3%) to 63 out of 266 (23.7%). The frequency of the exposure played a role in this study. When words were only encountered once, very little meaning uptake seemed to have occurred. At 2–3 exposures, there was a noticeable meaning acquisition for verbs, but this did not occur for nouns until 4–5 occurrences. By about 10+ exposures, there seemed to be a noticeable rise in the learning of meaning. As for use, the grammatical mastery of nouns (i.e., knowledge of appropriate articles) increased from 18 out of 140 (12.9%) to 60 out of 140 (42.9%); the grammatical knowledge of verbs (i.e., knowledge of appropriate prepositions) increased from 5 out of 126 (4%) to 26 out of 126 (20.6%). Thus, the acquisition of knowledge about which French articles accompany which nouns seem to be possible through reading. The knowledge of which prepositions accompany verbs, on the other hand, seemed to be acquired at a much slower rate.

Pigada and Schmitt (2006) also looked at the 133 words individually and examined which aspect of vocabulary knowledge (i.e., spelling, meaning, or grammar) was learned about them. They found that sixty-six (49.6%) were enhanced in one type of word knowledge, thirteen (9.8%) in two types, and eight (6%) in all three types. Adding the results together, Pigada and Schmitt

(2006) found that some degree of learning was demonstrated for 87 out of 133 words, a pick-up rate of 64.5 percent, or 1 word out of every 1.5 words tested. Thus, it is safe to conclude that ER led to the enhancement of knowledge about the spelling, meaning, and grammatical knowledge of words.

Horst (2005) assessed the vocabulary gains of twenty-one adult immigrant ESL learners at a community center in Montreal, Canada. The average number of books read by the twenty-one learners was 10.52 (SD = 6.71) over a six-week period, which means that students on average read 1.75 books per week. To create a pre-test, Horst (2005) scanned the first twenty pages from each of the twelve graded readers to create a pre-reading baseline test of words. The scanned files of graded readers were analyzed using VocabyProfile, an online version of the Lexical Frequency Profiling software developed by Nation and Heatley (1996). A 100-item pre-test with three rating options was prepared: No (*I don't know what this word means*); Not sure (*I have an idea about the meaning of this word, but I am not sure*); and Yes (*I know what this word means*). As many as 50 words were chosen from a 1,001–2,000-word frequency list and 50 words not appearing on lists of 2,000 most common word families (called off-list words). The post-tests were individualized, which were based on the graded readers read by each student. The 100-item post-tests were identical to the pre-test in format but were made up entirely of words known to have occurred in the books read by the participants. The result demonstrated the acquisition of full or partial knowledge in 51.43 percent of previously unknown words.

Recent ER research also supported impressive gains in vocabulary learning through enhanced ER, such as reading while listening (Webb et al., 2013; Webb & Chang, 2015) and ER-plus approach (i.e, ER was supplemented with post-reading discussion in small groups, Boutorwick et al., 2019). Webb and Chang (2015) suggested that with the availability of audio files in graded readers, reading while listening rather than reading alone should be "the primary approach" to extensive reading today (p. 682). Boutorwick et al. (2019) suggested that supplementing ER with discussion provided opportunities for further development of vocabulary knowledge.

In conclusion, the extensive body of research on ER strongly indicates its significant impact on vocabulary acquisition in language learning. Studies consistently demonstrate that ER facilitates incidental vocabulary learning, a process where learners gradually accumulate knowledge through repeated contextual encounters with words. This method has been proven effective not only in increasing the size of learners' vocabulary but also in enhancing their understanding of word meanings, usage, and even spelling. Furthermore, the effects of vocabulary learning through ER has been observed to be enhanced when combining ER with other approaches. These findings underscore the versatility and efficacy of ER as a tool to foster vocabulary acquisition among learners.

Points to Ponder
- Mention two post-reading activities that might enhance the learning of vocabulary through reading.
- How might you implement reading while listening to your own students?

3.3 Grammar

Not surprisingly, ER contributes to the learning of grammatical structures as has been demonstrated in both quantitative and qualitative studies (e.g., Aka, 2019, 2020; Lee et al., 2015; Nakano, 2023). While reading extensively with ease, students encounter a variety of grammatical patterns in contexts. The repeated exposure to grammatical structures from reading is cumulatively registered in the implicit learning system and as a result leads to incidental learning of grammar knowledge (Grabe, 2009). Research has shown that ER may play a more effective role in improving grammar knowledge than other methods such as explicit grammar instruction (e.g., Aka, 2019) or translation (Lee et al., 2015).

Adopting an experimental-control group design, Aka (2019) implemented ER among a group of 200 high school EFL learners in Japan. The control group ($n = 205$) had six English classes a week: 3 hours of intensive reading classes, 2 hours of grammar classes, and 1 hour of listening class. The ER group took the same number of English classes, but instead of two hours of grammar classes, this group took two hours of extensive reading classes. Students in the control group learned one grammar item each week and worked on grammar exercises. Students in the ER group were asked to select ER books at the i-1 level from a library of 3,000 graded readers. Thus, the only difference between the two groups was whether they had sixty hours of grammar instruction or ER over a course of one year. At the beginning of the experiment, the two groups did not significantly differ in their grammar and vocabulary knowledge measured by a proficiency test called BACE, however, the ER group performed significantly better in the grammar and vocabulary section of the test compared to the control group after one year. In a similar vein, Lee et al. (2015) compared the effects of two approaches, ER and translation, on knowledge of general grammar and specific syntactic features (i.e., articles and prepositions) among 124 middle school EFL learners in South Korea. The results showed that ER produced positive outcomes on grammar measures for high-level students.

A recent study also investigated the extent to which different ways of presenting grammatical information in graded readers influenced the incidental learning of grammatical knowledge (Nakano, 2023). The reading materials were two passages from JGR SAKURA, a website for L2 Japanese extensive reading that provides Japanese graded readers as well as one online Vocabulary Level Test for L2 Japanese. The study provided both graded readers with parts of speech being color-coded and normal texts for L2 learners at the elementary proficiency level. Compared to those reading normal texts, the participants who used the form-focused text (i.e., color-coded) tended to obtain higher scores in tests that assessed function word recognition and the relationship between modifiers and modified words. The results need to be interpreted with caution because only two texts were read in the study.

Frequency of exposure also plays a role in the incidental learning of grammar knowledge. Aka (2020) investigated the effects of reading on the incidental learning of a specific grammatical feature – *to-infinitives used as nouns* among 157 Japanese high school EFL learners. The experimental group ($n = 74$) read five passages consisting of a total of forty sentences that include to-infinitives used as nouns, while the control group ($n = 83$) also read five reading passages, but with only ten sentences consisting of to-infinitives used as nouns. The study showed that the experimental group participants noticed and learned about *to-infinitives used as nouns*. The study provided evidence that frequency of exposure contributed to the incidental learning of grammar.

In conclusion, the evidence from both quantitative and qualitative studies supports the notion that ER plays a crucial role in the incidental learning of grammatical structures for language learners. Through ER, students are repeatedly exposed to a variety of grammatical patterns in context, facilitating their absorption and understanding of these structures in a way that appears to be more effective than traditional methods like explicit grammar instruction or translation. These findings highlight the value of incorporating ER into language classrooms, not only for vocabulary development but also for enhancing students' grammatical competence more naturally and effectively.

Points to Ponder
- Would you incorporate ER in your teaching of grammar? Why or why not?

3.4 Writing

A good reader is also a good writer. Reading more is connected to better writing skills in both first (e.g., Sun et al., 2016) and second language (e.g., Park, 2016).

Empirical studies have shown that ER groups performed significantly better in key areas of writing compared to control groups (see Lee & Schallert, 2016; Mermelstein, 2015). This body of research examines the effects of ER on different aspects of writing, such as *task achievement, coherence and cohesion, lexical resource,* and *grammatical range and accuracy.* For example, Mermelstein's (2015) study investigated the extent to which an enhanced ER program improved the writing abilities of 211 third-year college EFL learners in Taiwan, China. ER was implemented as a sustained silent reading (SSR) activity, ranging from fifteen to twenty minutes. As many as 600 graded readers at Level 1 to Level 6 from the *Oxford Bookworms* and the *Penguin Readers* were available for the participants. The writing assignment was a descriptive paragraph writing, with "Your Past Summer Vacation" and "Your Future Summer Vacation" as topics for the pre- versus post-tests. The study showed that the ER group outperformed the control group in *vocabulary, language use, spelling/mechanics,* and *fluency of writing.*

A relationship between the amount of ER and writing achievement has also been established in research (e.g., Odo, 2020; Sakurai, 2017). For example, Sakurai (2017) investigated the relationship between the amount of extensive reading and the writing performance among 157 first and second-year EFL university students in an English language program at a private university in Japan. The students were taking English courses at different levels. ER was a component in some of the courses. Students needed to read 36,000 words and ER constituted 20 percent of the final grade in those courses. Some students were enrolled in a course that required them to read a minimum of 75,000 words. Students selected books from a library with over 12,000 ER books, read outside the classroom, and took quizzes on MReader. Students read 66,242 words on average. Based on the reading amount, the students were divided into four groups: Group 1: < 36,000 words; Group 2: 36,000–71,999 words; Group 3: 72,000–107,999 words; and Group 4: >108,000 words. The assessment of the writing was a letter-writing task. The participants were asked to write a letter of 150 words to a non-Japanese friend abroad about recent news in Japan and explain why Japanese people were interested in it. The grading rubric included *task achievement, coherence and cohesion, lexical resource,* and *grammatical range and accuracy* (see Appendix B in Sakurai, 2017, pp. 160–161). The results showed that the amount of reading was significantly correlated with the writing score total at 0.212 ($p < 0.01$). As for the four components of the writing rubric, the amount of ER was significantly correlated with *lexical resource* at 0.294 ($p < 0.001$) and *grammatical range and accuracy* at 0.246 ($p < 0.01$). In terms of the four groups, the group read more than 108,000 statistically outperformed the other three groups in *lexical resource* ($p < 0.001$) and *grammatical range and accuracy* ($p < 0.01$).

Additionally, the difficulty level of reading materials may influence writing quality. Odo (2020) revealed that more challenging ER materials were associated with greater writing class grade performance. However, there is a need for more studies to be conducted.

As for the genres of the writing, the studies have examined the effects of ER on letter writing (e.g., Sakurai, 2017), descriptive writing (Mermelstein, 2015), book reports (e.g., Kim & Ro, 2023; Sun, 2020), and academic writing (e.g., Park, 2016).

To conclude, current research has shown that the large amount of language input, together with opportunities to practice writing, contributes to different aspects of L2 writing ability in a variety of genres.

> **Points to Ponder**
> • How could you integrate ER into your future teaching practices to support and enhance your students' writing abilities?

3.5 Speaking

ER might promote speaking abilities in three ways. First, students learn oral expressions from ER books and then apply them in their speech. Many graded readers include dialogues, which demonstrates to learners how spoken language is produced. For example, in Zhou and Day (2021), EAP students mentioned using expressions learned from ER in their speaking. Second, ER, especially audio-assisted ER, has been shown to enhance students' pronunciation. Kirchhoff and Mision (2022) found that students enjoyed the reading while listening program (RWL) and felt it improved their pronunciation, prosody, and intonation. Third, ER-related activities, particularly speaking exercises, may enhance students' speaking abilities. L2 Chinese learners in Zhou and Day (2023) expressed that ER itself did not directly improve their speaking. However, their involvement in ER activities, such as summarizing stories they read to each other, teaching vocabulary, and describing drawings, significantly improved their speaking abilities.

> **Points to Ponder**
> • Why do you think reading extensively can improve learners' speaking abilities?
> • Design one or two post-reading activities to practice learners' speaking.

3.6 Reading Attitude

Alexandar and Filler (1976) defined reading attitude as "a system of feelings related to reading which causes the learner to approach or avoid a reading situation" (p. 1). Research has consistently shown that ER contributed to positive reading attitudes in an L2 (e.g., Habib & Watkins, 2023). After reviewing a list of reading attitude studies, Yamashita (2004) summarized that reading attitude contains three components: cognitive (*personal, evaluative beliefs*), affective (*feelings and emotions*), and conative (*action readiness and behavioral intentions*). Day and Bamford (1998) claimed that four factors might affect L2 reading attitude:

- L1 reading attitude
- previous experience with learning to read other second languages
- attitudes toward the L2, culture and people
- the L2 classroom environment such as teachers, classmates, and ongoing experience in L2 reading.

Empirically, Yamashita (2004) investigated the relationship between L1 (Japanese) and L2 (English) reading attitudes and ER performance among fifty-nine Japanese EFL university students. A factorial analysis revealed four components of reading attitude: *comfort* (i.e., positive feeling), *anxiety* (negative feeling), *value* (i.e., values of reading), and *self-perception* (i.e., students' perceptions of themselves as readers). It was found that *values* of reading in L1 and L2 are significantly correlated ($r = 0.629$). *Anxiety* in reading is higher in L2 than in L1, *comfort* in reading is higher in L1 than L2, the *value* that the students attached to reading does not differ between L1 and L2, and *self-perception* as a reader is more positive in L1 than in L2. Among the two affective variables, anxiety and comfort, only comfort was significantly correlated with ER performance measured by the number of pages read. This indicates that positive feelings facilitated ER, highlighting the role of positive feelings in enhancing reading attitude. As the author claimed, experiencing a positive feeling is more motivational than not experiencing a negative feeling (Yamashita, 2004).

The relationship between ER and reading attitude seems to be a reciprocal one. Zhou and Day (2021) revealed that fifty-seven EAP students' reading attitude was significantly improved after an online ER program lasting for ten to twelve weeks. Mohd Asraf and Ahmad (2003) showed that students in rural schools in Malaysia developed positive attitudes toward reading in English after four months of Guided Extensive Reading.

L2 learners, including advanced ones, often experience feelings of anxiety, fear, and reluctance toward reading in a foreign or second language, as reported in studies like Tabata-Sandom (2023). Comfort and enjoyment while reading in their L2 are less common among these learners, often due to various factors such as the difficulty of the reading materials or reading primarily to learn vocabulary and grammar (e.g., Ro, 2013). ER, as an innovative approach to language teaching, offers L2 learners the opportunity to enjoy reading and develop a habit of it.

> **Points to Ponder**
> - What factors can influence learners' attitudes to reading in a foreign language?
> - How might reading teachers effectively address and mitigate negative feelings such as anxiety and fear toward reading in a foreign language to foster a more positive reading attitude?

3.7 Reading Motivation

Motivation plays an important role in successful foreign or second language reading. Day and Bamford (1998) defined motivation as "what makes people do (or not do) something" (p. 27). As we have discussed in the previous section, reading attitude is about positive or negative feelings toward reading. Motivation, however, goes a step further by serving as a prerequisite for actual reading behavior. It directly or indirectly influences the amount of reading and the time devoted to ER, as suggested by Mori (2002). Research on motivation and ER has consistently shown a strong positive relationship between the two (Robb & Ewert, 2024).

Day and Bamford explained the motivation to read in an L2 through the Expectancy Value model (p. 28). The Expectancy Value Model is composed of four variables: (a) materials, (b) reading ability in the L2, (c) attitude toward reading in the L2, and (d) sociocultural environment. Day and Bamford claimed that (a) materials and (c) attitude toward reading in the L2 are the critical components of reading motivation.

Empirical research has provided evidence for Day and Bamford's Expectancy Value model (e.g., Tabata-Sandom, 2023; Takase, 2007). For example, studies have reported that providing appropriate reading materials was a crucial factor in motivating L2 learners to read (Bui & Macalister, 2021; Takase, 2007). The books' intriguing contents motivated students to form the reading habit (Bui & Macalister, 2021).

Noticing an improvement in language abilities will motivate students to read. For example, students in Bui and Macalister (2021) reported that reading online promoted their reading fluency and vocabulary knowledge, thus this observed improvement in their reading abilities was an incentive for them to maintain their reading habits.

Takase (2007) identified a list of components of L1 and L2 reading motivation among a group of female Japanese high school EFL learners. Their parents' involvement in and family attitudes toward reading was one of the components.

This demonstrates that sociocultural factors such as parents, teachers, and classmates all play a role in motivating students to read or not.

Zhou and Day (2023) showed that positive attitudes toward L2 reading (e.g., confidence) may motivate students to continue reading and taking Chinese classes. It is safe to say that motivation to read is influenced by reading materials, L2 reading abilities, contextual factors, as well as attitudes toward L2 reading.

It is worth noting that motivation for ER is not static, but complex and dynamic (de Burgh-Hirabe & Feryok, 2013). It is dynamic because the motivation for ER can increase or decrease. For example, in de Burgh-Hirabe and Feryok (2013), nine L2 Japanese learners from two high schools in a New Zealand city were encouraged to read extensively outside class for five to seven months. Motivation for ER changed for seven of the nine participants. The motivation of four students increased, three students decreased, and two students remained stable. Research has also shown that readers may start to read with extrinsic motivation, which can be transferred to intrinsic motivation when reading tasks are intriguing (e.g., Demirci, 2019).

Motivation is also complex (e.g., de Burgh-Hirabe & Feryok, 2013; de Lozier, 2019; Ro, 2018; Robb & Ewert, 2024). Diverse internal and external factors may enhance or hinder learners' commitment to ER (Robb & Ewert, 2024). de Burgh-Hirabe and Feryok's study (2013) showed motivation to read in L2 Japanese was influenced by multiple factors, including *students' attitudes about Japanese language and culture, their beliefs about L2 learning, their perceived success in ER, their workload at school, their social relationships* and so on. Motivation to read may also vary among learners with different proficiency levels, for example, high- and intermediate-level learners versus low-level readers (de Lozier, 2019). The former group performed better and enjoyed reading more under intrinsic conditions while the latter benefited more from extrinsic motivational requirements.

Research has revealed that individual readers can apply regulation strategies to increase their motivation to read (e.g., Arnold, 2009; de Burgh-Hirabe & Feryok, 2013; Li et al., 2023). This ability is called self-regulation, the self-directive processes and self-beliefs that enable learners to transform mental abilities into academic performance skills (Zimmerman, 2008, p. 166). Two examples are learners in de Burgh-Hirabe and Feryok's study (2013) who regulated the challenges posed by the books (e.g., reading challenging books) as well as the environment (e.g., allocating time for ER). Li et al. (2023) showed that students with high self-directed learning abilities significantly increased their reading amount and days than those with low self-directed learning abilities while doing online ER on *BookRoll*, a digital teaching material distribution system developed by Kyoto University.

As has been discussed, motivation decides whether students want to read, how much they read, and how long they spend on reading. The experience of reading extensively in a foreign language, on the other hand, can promote reading motivation. Ro (2013) examined the extent to which ER motivated an L2 reader Liza (pseudonym), a twenty-eight-year-old Korean female, in twenty-four extensive reading sessions over an eight-week period. Liza's motivation was enhanced through ER due to the influence of the following factors (*comfort or ease, enjoyment, satisfaction, convenience or accessibility,* and *usefulness*). Liza felt comfort or ease in comprehension from exposure to repeated use of the same words or phrases, no pressure for reading, and familiarity with the background and storyline of the books. Another factor that increased reading motivation was enjoyment experienced while reading (i.e., *enjoyment in reading comics* and *enjoyment in reading the colloquial expressions*). Liza also experienced satisfaction after finishing reading English books, which motivated her to purchase more L2 comics and read more.

In language classrooms, some readers may not have intrinsic motivation for ER when they first get into contact with it. However, extrinsic motivation (e.g., easy to get credits) could be transformed into intrinsic motivation as has been demonstrated in some studies (e.g., Arai, 2022; Mori, 2015). The phenomenon is supported by the concept of emergent motivation (Csikszentmihalyi et al., 2005). Gamification features like leaderboards, prizes, progress bars, star system, avatar builder, badges, raz-rockets, and certificates can also be incorporated into the design of ER programs to enhance motivation to read, especially among young learners (e.g., Grade 2 to 5 L1 Korean EFL learners in Jun, 2018; Grade 5 to 6 primary school students in Iraq, Bala, 2022). Book review activity through *Bibliobattles* (a social book review game) combines silent reading and public sharing of books, which also enhances motivation to read (Maclauchlan, 2018). Robb and Ewert (2024) also explored additional strategies and incentives to motivate readers, such as reading marathons, book sharing, and quizzes, among others. Teachers should also pay attention to the fluctuation of students' motivation toward ER (Mikami, 2017). Without maintaining and actively enhancing students' motivation to read, it will be very difficult to keep students engaged in ER over an extended period of time.

In summary, the role of motivation in ER is both critical and multifaceted, influencing learners' willingness to read, the amount of reading they undertake, and the duration of their engagement with ER. Empirical research underscores that motivation for ER is not static but dynamic and complex, subject to changes and influenced by a myriad of factors, including material appropriateness, reading ability, attitude toward L2 reading, and the socio-cultural environment. Studies have shown that motivation can evolve from extrinsic to intrinsic, especially when the reading material is engaging. It is important for language teachers to recognize and address the fluctuating nature of motivation to ensure sustained engagement in ER, thereby maxi-mizing its benefits.

Points to Ponder
- How can teachers keep students interested and motivated to read more, especially when it comes to reading in a new language?

3.8 Reading Habit

Reading habit has been a topic of interest in many ER studies. It was defined as "how often, how well, and what adults like to read" (Scales & Rhee, 2001, p. 178). In Rodrigo et al.'s (2014) study, it was operationalized as how frequently the participants read novels, whether they read the entire book, and whether they engage in literacy-related activities such as visiting book-stores or libraries. Positive reading attitude is an important factor in the development of a reading habit. Since ER has been shown to enhance reading attitudes, it also contributes to the forming of a reading habit.

Rodrigo et al. (2014) investigated the effects of two reading interventions, one ER group and another non-ER group, on the reading habits of 181 adults with low literacy skills. The study showed that the participants in the ER group developed more of an ability to finish reading a whole book compared to the participants in the non-ER group. As for bookstore and library visits, the ER group and the non-ER group did not differ before the treatment. However, after the treatment, the ER group visited bookstores and libraries statistically more often than participants in the non-ER group. As expected, the ER group read statistically more books compared to the non-ER group. Furthermore, what is worth noting is that participants in the ER group, six months after treatment, were still reading more books than those in the non-ER group. Thus, it was concluded that the ER intervention was more effect-ive in promoting a reading habit (Rodrigo et al., 2014).

Setting a reading requirement such as how many words, pages, or books students need to read has been shown to help the formation of a reading habit. For example, Zhou and Day (2021) required EAP students in an English language institute in an American university to read 10,000 to 12,000 words per week. One interviewee said "Until I really try reading it, so I say, this is good, so I made a habit to read it" and he "reads every week" (p. 14). Teachers' guidance and scaffolding also promote the forming of a reading habit. Tabata-Sandom (2023) regularly sent newsletters to her advanced L2 learners to recommend books and encourage each participant. This "soft enforcement" helped the participants to commit to the ER program.

In conclusion, the development of a reading habit is a key focus in ER, with studies indicating that ER significantly contributes to the formation of a reading habit. The research findings so far collectively underscore the value of ER in not just improving reading skills but also in instilling a lasting appreciation and practice of reading.

Points to Ponder
- Apart from being a fluent reader, what are other benefits of a good reading habit for L2 learners?
- How can language teachers cultivate a good reading habit among readers?

3.9 Flow Experience

Flow theory emerged from the work of Csikszentmihalyi (1988) researching humans' optimal or most enjoyable experiences. Engeser and Schiepe-Tiska (2012) defined flow as a perceived state in which "an individual is completely immersed in an activity without reflective self-consciousness but with a deep sense of control" (p. 1). Analysis from a variety of people in different professions and cultures revealed similar explanations of life's most enjoyable experiences, that is, an intense focus on a task. When in the flow state, people focus their intention completely on what they are doing. Their action and consciousness are being sufficiently merged that they lose their self-consciousness (Nakamura & Csikszentmihalyi, 2009).

According to Csikszentmihalyi (1988), conditions for a flow experience included clear goals, feedback, skills matching challenges, an environment to concentrate, and an element to control. Kirchhoff (2013, p. 199) mentioned that the five conditions that allow for flow experience to occur are quite similar to the principles and practices of ER (see Table 3).

It is hard to become immersed in an activity when one does not know what needs to be done (i.e., clear goals) and how well one is doing (i.e., immediate feedback). ER programs usually set clear goals for students. For example, L2 Chinese learners in Zhou and Day (2023) were required to read one graded reader per week. Advanced, post-tertiary L2 English learners in Tabata-Sandom (2023) agreed to read fifteen minutes per day, and that reading amount is "the contract" (p. 172). Day and Bamford (1998) recommended students in ER

Table 3 Conditions of flow and elements of extensive reading approach
(adapted from Kirchhoff, 2013).

Conditions of flow	Elements of ER
Clear goals	The goal is to read for pleasure, general understanding, and fun
Immediate feedback	A sense of accomplishment in following a story or completing a book
Skills match challenges	Read level-appropriate books
Focused concentration	Silent reading time in the classroom or other locations
Control is possible	Learners decide what, where, and how to read

programs read one book per week. Thus, it seems that it would be beneficial to set up clear reading goals in ER programs. ER also gave students real-time feelings as feedback so it encouraged them to read consistently for its own sake (Fongpaiboon, 2017).

People also reported focused concentration when involved in enjoyable activities. Attention was reported to be completely immersed in the activity at hand, so that the "merging of activity and awareness" is a typical feature of the flow experience (Csikszentmihalyi, 1988, p. 32). One reader in Tabata-Sandom (2023) said, "When a story is interesting, one hour feels like a second, even if it's in English" (p. 172). Because of the deep concentration on the activity at hand, the results of flow experience include temporarily losing the awareness of self, forgetting problems in life or work, lacking self-consciousness (Kirchhoff, 2013) and even experiencing a "transcendence of self," caused by the unusually high involvement in an action (Csikszentmihalyi, 1988, p. 33).

The universal precondition for flow is that a person "should perceive that there is something for him or her to do, and that he or she is capable of doing it" (Csikszentmihalyi, 1988, p. 30). In other words, flow or optimal experience requires *a balance between the challenges and the skills* a person brings to it. Csikszentmihalyi (1988) gave an example of playing tennis. When a tennis player plays tennis and feels enjoyment, he/she wants to play more. The more such individuals play, the better their skills will be. If they continue to play against opponents of the same level as before, they will feel bored. To return to flow and replicate the enjoyment, they have to play with stronger opponents. Thus, to maintain the flow, one must increase the complexity of the activity by "developing new skills and taking on new challenges" (Kirchhoff, 2013, p. 30). This dynamic and spiraling complexity is what makes flow a process of "discovering something new" (p. 30).

Flow pushes people to stretch themselves, take on new challenges, and sharpen their skills. Participants in Tabata-Sandom (2023) reported flow experience when they started reading higher-level, longer books. Arai (2022) investigated the relationship between perceived book difficulty and flow experience. The survey results showed that the participants reading "*i* plus 1" books had higher total scores on the flow scale than those who read "*i* minus 1" ones. The study suggested that many participants found flow in their reading and that ER was a "flow-generating" activity (p. 16). This finding is especially relevant to book selection. Some students may tend to read and stay at easy and low levels. However, they could be encouraged to select books that match their reading abilities.

Empirical research has also been conducted on the flow experience in ER programs. For example, Kirchhoff (2013) investigated the occurrences of flow experience from two groups of Japanese college students (seventy-two in total) in extensive reading classes. The extensive reading class met once a week for ninety minutes and continued for fifteen weeks. Every class included thirty minutes of silent reading time and other activities such as repeated reading tasks or discussion about books with classmates. Flow experience was mentioned in relation to book selection, with the purpose of encouraging students to select books that are at the readers' levels so that the books are not too boring or too challenging. Students were also encouraged to read at least an hour outside class. The questionnaires asked for frequency of flow-like experiences, descriptions of conditions that enabled flow, reading speed, amount of reading accomplished, L1 reading flow experience, and specific elements of flow experiences. The results revealed that the participants reported flow-like experiences when reading graded readers. The study suggested that teachers can facilitate the flow experience by providing books that are interesting to students and at the students' reading levels, and by encouraging students to read in a calm and relaxing environment.

Fongpaiboon (2017) investigated the flow experience of sixty-eight Thai undergraduate students from doing ER for one semester. The study explored both the external and internal conditions for flow experience to occur. The results revealed that a quiet, calm, and relaxing environment, being able to select reading materials, and intriguing reading content were the top three ranked external conditions to enable flow experience. The interview data showed that the self-selection of ER materials helped students visualize or imagine while reading the stories and enabled flow experience. For example, one of the interviewees said:

> I was engrossed in some types of reading materials that I like so I could visualize the story as if I was in the book and that made me feel enjoyment, happy, and I would like to read more. (p. 71)

To conclude, as Grabe stated, the concept of flow provides a strong rationale for promoting ER, both in and out of the classroom (2009). The characteristics of ER of being able to read intriguing, level-appropriate materials for general understanding and enjoyment encouraged participants to experience flow through the power of making reading decisions by readers.

Points to Ponder
- Give an example of a time when you experienced flow while reading in a foreign language.
- Reflecting on the concept of flow and its relation to ER, how can language teachers create a classroom environment that fosters flow experiences for learners?

4 ER across Languages

4.1 English

In this section, I mainly present descriptive statistics of the number of ER studies conducted in EFL/ESL contexts from 2018 to 2023. I will not describe individual studies in EFL/ESL contexts because many examples have been provided in Section 3. The data source is from the Extensive Reading Foundation's annotated bibliography of works on ER (https://bib.erfounda tion.org). The main reason is that the bibliography is a comprehensive collection of the ER studies published in different journals, including *Reading in a Foreign Language*, *Journal of Extensive Reading*, *The Reading Matrix,* and other international and local journals. The annotated bibliography also included dissertations, MA theses and discussion pieces on ER. The focus of this analysis primarily rests on ER studies published in English. This is due to limitations in my language proficiency, time, and available space, which may preclude the comprehensive inclusion of studies published in other languages.

Day and Bamford (1998) published their seminal book on ER in 1998, thus papers published in and after 1998 were perceived to reflect the nature of ER and followed the top ten ER principles to a different extent. Thus, I searched and downloaded all the studies collected in the database published in and after 1998. The search resulted in 644 studies. Due to the limited space, this section only reported the data for the last five years, from 2018 to 2023. I hope readers can gain an understanding of the most recent trends in ER research and practices.

As many as 175 ER studies were published from 2018 to 2023. An initial reading of the papers showed that thirty-three studies were not related to ER (e.g., on extensive listening, vocabulary learning through reading, reading models

Table 4 Descriptive statistics of ER studies conducted from 2018 to 2023.

Context	Number of studies	Percentage
EFL	88	83.02%
ESL	5	4.72%
L2 English[a]	3	2.83%
French as a foreign language	1	0.94%
Chinese as a foreign language	1	0.94%
Spanish	1	0.94%
Italian	1	0.94%
Japanese as a second language	2	1.89%
Japanese as a foreign language	2	1.89%
Norwegian as an additional language[b]	1	0.94%
English as a third language	1	0.94%
Total	106	100%

[a] L2 English refers to studies that included both EFL and ESL participants (e.g., Tabata-Sandom, 2023) or did not specify whether it was EFL or ESL context.
[b] Norwegian as an additional language: Two participants in Krulatz and Duggan (2018) were multilingual speakers and both spoke four to five languages. Thus, Norwegian was labeled an additional language in this analysis.

review). Thus, those studies were not included in this analysis. Thirty-six studies from 2018 to 2023 were related to ER (e.g., discussion of ER implementation issues, Renandya et al., 2021; ER website review, Alzahrani, 2022), but they are not empirical studies. Thus, those studies were not included in the analysis.

Table 4 presents the number of empirical ER studies conducted from 2018 to 2023. Around 106 empirical studies on ER were published from 2018 to 2023, among which eighty-eight (83.02%) were conducted in EFL contexts, five studies (4.72%) in ESL contexts, and three studies did not specify whether it was an ESL or EFL context. Only one study was conducted in French as a foreign language, Chinese as a foreign language, L2 Spanish, L2 Italian, and Norwegian as an additional language, respectively. Four studies were conducted in L2 Japanese. Thus, we can conclude that the majority of ER studies were conducted in EFL contexts.

The studies conducted in EFL/ESL contexts investigated a variety of topics in ER, including but not limited to attitude (e.g., Birketveit et al., 2018; Endris, 2018; Park, 2020), motivation (e.g., Al Damen, 2018; de Lozier, 2019; Demirci, 2019; Tusmagambet, 2020), reading fluency (Tragant Mestres et al., 2019; Tusmagambet, 2020), vocabulary (Aliyar & Peters, 2022; Bourtorwick et al., 2019; Sakurai, 2023; Stoeckel et al., 2021), reading comprehension (Lyddon &

Kramer, 2019; Shimono, 2023), self-efficacy (McLean & Poulshock, 2018), reading amount (Jun, 2018; McLean & Poulshock, 2018) and so on.

The studies conducted in EFL contexts were carried out in a variety of countries and among learners speaking different L1s, such as Japanese (Arai, 2022; Klassen & Allan, 2019; Klassen & Green, 2019; Kramer & McLean, 2019; Sakurai, 2023; Shimono, 2023), Amharic (Endris, 2018), Korean (Ro, 2018), Mandarin Chinese (Shih et al., 2018), Arabic (Abdulrahman & Kara, 2023; Al Damen, 2018), Indonesian (Zulfariati, 2023), Emirati (Demirci, 2019), Kazakh (Tusmagambet, 2020), Norwegian (Birketveit et al., 2018), and so on.

Points to Ponder
- Please select an ER study of your choice, carefully read through it, and then create a concise summary of its key findings and insights. Share your summary and discuss its implications with a classmate.

4.2 Chinese

Chinese is a logographic writing system and reading in Chinese may cause anxiety, especially among readers whose L1 is an alphabetical language (Zhou, 2017). Chinese differ from English in many ways. First, the basic graphic form in Chinese is the character. Each character corresponds to a syllable and carries meaning. Chinese characters function as the basic units in Chinese reading (e.g., Zhou, 2023). Each character is composed of strokes, which are combined to form radicals. There are two types of radicals in Chinese, semantic and phonetic radicals. The former provides information on the meaning of the character while the latter provides hints to its pronunciation. L1 and L2 Chinese reading research has shown that radical knowledge increases with years of language learning and there is a strong relationship between radical knowledge and character recognition (e.g., Shen & Ke, 2007; Zhou, 2023). Second, Chinese employs compounding as an effective and productive way of word formation (Zhou, 2021). The compounding process allows two or even three morphemes (Chinese characters) to form a compound word. According to the Modern Chinese Frequency Dictionary, disyllabic words (e.g., two-charatcer/morpheme words) compose 74 percent of the total corpus of commonly used words (cf. Shen & Ke, 2007). The two characters in a compound word form a quasi-syntactic relationship with each other. Yip (2000) identified five types of relationships commonly found in Chinese disyllabic words: juxtopositional, modificational, governmental, predicational, and complemental. Research has shown that morphological awareness directly contributed to vocabulary knowledge in Chinese reading and indirectly contributed to Chinese reading through the mediation of vocabulary knowledge (e.g., Zhou, 2021). Third, unlike English which is an inflectional language, there are few explicit syntactic or grammatical markers in Chinese (e.g., Zhou, 2022). As a result, Chinese readers rely on their syntactic knowledge such as word order to solicit information about tense, parts of speech, and so on. Taking the features of the Chinese language into consideration, researchers called for providing more opportunities for students to read extensively in Chinese (e.g., Zhou, 2018).

Compared to studies in EFL and ESL contexts, there is a scarcity of research on ER in L2 Chinese, for example, Chinese as a foreign language (CFL) or Chinese as a second language, (CSL) contexts. This does not mean that ER programs have not been set up in L2 Chinese contexts. When I was a PhD student at the University of Hawai'i at Manoa, the Chinese flagship housed in the East Asian Language and Literatures Department had an ER library, and students learning Chinese were encouraged to read extensively. A recent publication by me and Dr. Richard Day reported the establishment of an ER program in a CFL context. The ER program was established in an American liberal arts college.

An important step in establishing an ER program was to build an ER library (Day & Bamford, 2002). An ER library with approximately 200 books was set up for the Chinese ER program. The books were all graded readers, mainly from the Chinese Breeze graded readers series (Liu & Chu, 2008). The books were labeled into three levels according to the number of headwords of each book: Level S (150 headwords), Level 1 (300 headwords), and Level 2 (500 headwords).

The program was run from 2018 to 2022 and went through many changes. For example, ER was changed to an online format during the pandemic and the reading amount was also adjusted based on students' feedback. Students were required to read one book per week, as suggested by Day and Bamford (2002). A total of 5 percent of the final grade was assigned to ER. Students were required to read both in class and outside of the class. Class time was also allocated to ER activities.

Zhou and Day (2023) mainly investigated the effects of ER on L2 Chinese reading attitude, students' perceptions of language abilities being improved, and their views of ER activities.

The factorial analysis of the reading attitude survey showed a five-factor structure: *confidence, enjoyment, interest, practical value,* and *devotion.* It was found that L2 Chinese learners differed in their reading attitude before and after reading extensively for one semester. *Confidence* and *devotion* were two reading attitude components being improved significantly. The effect sizes of confidence $d = 0.66$ and devotion $d = 0.35$ indicated that L2 Chinese learners had 0.66 and 0.35 standard deviations of more *confidence in reading in Chinese* and *devotion to learning the Chinese language* after reading ten ER books for one semester. The end-of-the-semester final reflection showed that 86 percent of the learners enjoyed ER. They reported that the reading materials were interesting, fun, and out of the ordinary. Moreover, ER made them more confident, and they learned about Chinese culture through reading.

As for the language abilities perceived to have been improved, the students reported that reading speed (twenty-three times), reading comprehension (twenty-one times), vocabulary (twenty times), grammar (eighteen times), writing (nine times), character and word inferencing (seven times), character recognition (four times), listening (three times), and speaking (three times) were all improved. The number in the parenthesis indicated the frequency of that language ability mentioned by the forty-one participants. Two language abilities are specifically related to learning Chinese: character and word inferencing and character recognition. Participants noted that they became more capable of dealing with unknown characters by using contextual clues or simply skipping unknown characters.

L2 Chinese learners in Zhou and Day (2023) were asked to complete ER activities, which were adapted from Bamford and Day (2004). Some of the activities were more traditional ones such as the Instant Book Report, while others were more creative ones, such as Gifts (to give main characters gifts) and My Story (Students create their own stories). Please see Zhou and Day (2023, p. 229, Table 3) for the complete list of the ER activities and their descriptions.

One of the activities in *The Story and Drawing* asked students to fill in the basic information about the stories they read, then to draw pictures based on the stories, to write briefly about the pictures and what happened in the story before and after the picture, and express their opinions of the stories. Figures 1 and 2

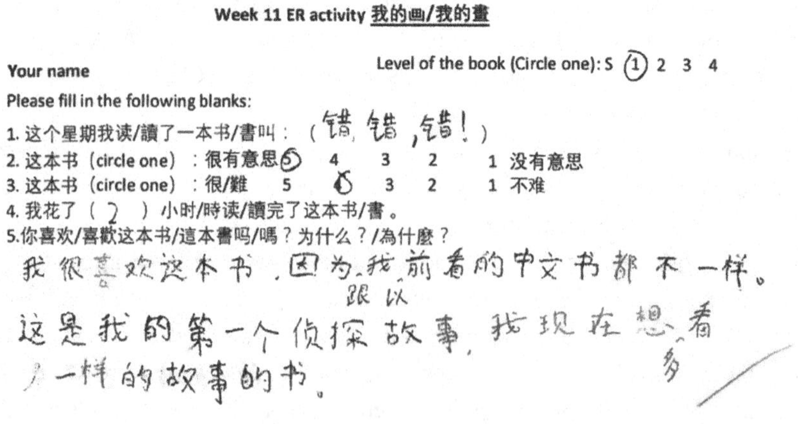
Week 11 ER activity 我的画/我的畫

Your name Level of the book (Circle one): S (1) 2 3 4

Please fill in the following blanks:

1. 这个星期我读/讀了一本书/書叫：（错，错，错！）
2. 这本书（circle one）：很有意思 (5) 4 3 2 1 没有意思
3. 这本书（circle one）：很/難 5 (4) 3 2 1 不难
4. 我花了（2）小时/時读/讀完了这本书/書。
5. 你喜欢/喜歡这本书/這本書吗/嗎？为什么？/為什麼？

我很喜欢这本书，因为跟以前看的中文书都不一样。这是我的第一个侦探故事，我现在想看多一样的故事的书。

Figure 1 ER activity – *The Story and Drawing* – Part 1 book report.

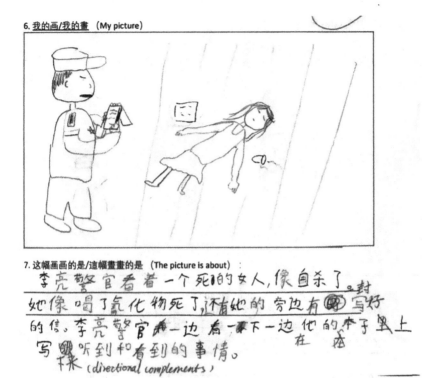

6. 我的画/我的畫 （My picture）

7. 这幅画画的是/這幅畫畫的是 （The picture is about）：
李亮警官看着一个死的女人，像自杀了。对
她像喝了氰化物死了，还有她的旁边有🔲写好
的信。李亮警官一边看一下一边他的本子上
写👐听到和看到的事情。
在   在
（directional complements）

Figure 2 A student's drawing of the story *Cuo Cuo Cuo* and a brief explanation
of the drawing – Part 2.

Note. The description of the drawing in English: Officer Li Liang looks at a dead woman.
It seems like she committed suicide. It appears she died from drinking cyanide. Also,
there is a letter written next to her, and Officer Li writes down in his notebook everything
he sees and hears.

are examples of one student's work for the activity *The Story and Drawing*. This
student read a Level 1 book. The name of the book is 错错错 (*Wrong, Wrong,
Wrong*). It is from the Chinese Breeze graded readers series by Liu and Chu
(2008) published by Beijing University Press. This student thought this book
was very interesting (5 out of 5). As for the difficulty level, 4 was selected, so it
seemed that the book was challenging for this student. It took the student
two hours to complete reading this book. As for the reasons why this student
liked the book, it was stated, "I really like this book, because it is different from
all the Chinese books I read before. It is the first detective story I read in
Chinese, and I would like to read more stories of this genre."

Here is another example of a story read by one student (see Figure 3). The
name of the book is *Shennong Tasting a Hundred Herbs*. Shennong, also known
as the Divine Farmer, is a legendary figure in Chinese mythology and is one of

6. 我的画/我的畫 (My picture)

7. 这幅画画的是/這幅畫畫的是 (The picture is about) :

Figure 3 Another student's drawing of an ER book *Shennong Tasting a Hundred Herbs*.

Note. The description of the drawing in English: The leader found a leaf that could help him. When he had a stomachache, eating this medicine made him feel better.

the ancient Chinese cultural heroes. He is credited with the invention of agriculture and traditional Chinese medicine. According to legend, Shennong tasted various herbs to determine their medicinal properties, thereby identifying poisonous plants and herbs that could be used for healing. Legend also says Shennong discovered tea when leaves from a wild tea tree blew into his pot of boiling water. This tale highlights his contribution to the development of herbal medicine in ancient China. The student draws the main character Shennong and the caption says "I can help the people in my tribe!" (Figure 3).

Another engaging activity is *My Story*. Students were encouraged to write their own stories, bring them to class, and share them with their peers. Those stories can also be used as reading materials for future students. The following story (see Table 5) written by a student talks about his experience driving bicycles in Shanghai.

Although one of the top ten ER principles is reading for its own sake (Day & Bamford, 2002), previous research has demonstrated the benefits of ER activities (e.g., Zhou & Day, 2021). In Zhou and Day (2023), 70 percent of the participants stated that they enjoyed ER activities. Five reasons contributed to

Table 5 ER activity – My story.

我在上海骑自行车

我上高二以后的暑假, 去了上海一个月。在上海我住在一个寄宿家庭的家里, 每天去实习。我的寄宿家庭住得离复旦大学很近, 可是我的实习工作离寄宿家庭有一点儿远。我每天需要骑二十分钟的自行车去地铁站, 然后坐一个小时的地铁去实习。在上海骑自行车非常害怕。上海的街很拥挤, 有很多车, 很多人, 太麻烦了!

在上海的大街上, 很多人卖东西, 比如说衣服, 菜, 日用品什么的。我的寄宿家庭告诉我不应该从哪里买吃的, 因为我可能会得病。可是, 有一天我买了一些小笼包。我觉得这是我吃过的最好吃的小笼包了。

虽然我觉得在上海的街上骑自行车有一点儿麻烦, 可是一个月以后每天骑自行车成为了我的习惯。我非常喜欢住在上海的一个月, 也喜欢每天骑自行车。我骑自行车的时候可以看到, 闻到, 听到, 感受到上海。我希望我将来一天回到上海去。

English translation:

Riding bicycles in Shanghai

During the summer break after my sophomore year in high school, I spent a month in Shanghai. I stayed with a host family and interned daily. My host family lived close to Fudan University, but my internship was a bit far from their home. I had to bike for twenty minutes to the subway station and then take an hour-long subway ride to my internship. Biking in Shanghai was very scary. The streets were crowded with many cars and people, making it quite troublesome!

In the streets of Shanghai, many people sold things like clothes, vegetables, and daily necessities. My host family advised me not to buy food from certain places to avoid getting sick. However, one day I bought some Xiaolongbao, which I thought was the most delicious food I had ever tasted.

Although I found biking on the streets of Shanghai to be a bit of a hassle, it became a habit after a month. I really enjoyed my month living in Shanghai and biking every day. Biking allowed me to see, smell, hear, and feel Shanghai. I hope to return to Shanghai one day.

Note. More stories written by students can be found on the IChineseER website under Topic "Story by Students" (https://lchineseer.sites.pomona.edu/tag/story-by-students/).

their enjoyment, including *providing activities to interact with classmates, solidifying comprehension, a variety of activities, different from normal classroom activities*, and *forcing them to read*. For example, one student claimed:

The ER activities are very helpful because it forces you to actually do the readings. College students are very busy and it can be easy to sometimes forget to read the book at times. Also, ER activity is a nice change of pace from normal classroom activities and is a more fun alternative to just learning material on a PowerPoint. (Excerpt 11 in Zhou & Day, 2023, p. 238)

Another student stated:

I did enjoy the ER activities. They weren't too stressful and allowed us to effectively show what we had learned. Earlier, I said that the extensive reading itself didn't aid my listening or speaking skills. However, I'd say that the activities definitely did. I found facilitating and understanding conversation to be much easier towards the end of the semester. I also appreciate the fact that the activities were different every week as well. (Excerpt 13 in Zhou & Day, 2023, p. 239)

It is understandable that some students did not like ER activities. One of the reasons mentioned was the sharing in the class was rushed, which is under-standable because they only had ten to fifteen minutes to share as a group. Another reason mentioned was it was not possible for students to know how to pronounce unknown characters without looking up the pronunciation. Since Chinese characters only include partial information about their pronunciations (through phonetic radicals), learners need to look up the dictionary if they really want to know how to pronounce a certain character. Thus, for a logographic language like Chinese, listening while reading may be worth trying.

To gather more feedback from students, teachers can ask students to write a reflection at the semester's end. In the Chinese ER program, I prompted students to reflect by answering six specific questions. This method enables teachers to collect students' feedback and subsequently enhance the program. Figure 4 showcases a reflection from a student in my Intermediate Chinese class.

Though there are not too many published studies on ER in L2 Chinese context, it does not mean that enthusiastic language teachers are not implement-ing one or another form of ER in their teaching. Reading materials or websites have also been published or developed by publishers or language practitioners. The following is a list of online ER reading resources for L2 Chinese learners.

- The Chairman's Bao (https://www.thechairmansbao.com)
- Ponddy Reader (https://ponddy-reader.netlify.app) (see Zhou & Zhao, 2023 for the website review)
- Dada Chinese (https://dd-la.com/)
- Du Chinese (https://www.duchinese.net/lessons)
- HSK Reading (https://hskreading.com/)
- IChineseER (https://lchineseer.sites.pomona.edu)
- Mandarin Bean (https://mandarinbean.com)

Mandarin Companion published graded readers in three levels: break-through (150 Chinese characters), Level 1 (300 Chinese characters), and

ER Reading Reflection
3 December 2018

1. Do you love reading in your native language? Why or why not?
I love reading in my native language. Especially when I was younger, I would read every single day; I would become engrossed in the stories and wouldn't be able to put down the book. As I grew busier with school I had less and less time to read, but I still enjoy doing so when I get the chance.

2. What was your reading experience before taking Chinese 51A?
I had not read many books in Chinese prior to Chinese 51A. In class we read quite a few shorter pieces, similar to the text we use in class, but the only book we read was "The Lady in the Painting."

3. Did you enjoy Extensive Reading this semester? Why or why not?
I enjoyed Extensive Reading a lot. It was fun to have a new story to read every week, and all of the books that I read were very different from each other so it was fun to see the contrast. While I had heard some of the stories before, others were very new to me, so it was interesting to see where those stories led.

4. What aspects of your Chinese language abilities do you think have been improved through doing Extensive Reading?
I think that the aspects of my Chinese language abilities that have improved the most through extensive reading is my reading speed and reading comprehension. By reading a lot and attempting to read relatively quickly, I think I improved my ability to understand sentences based on the context even if I did not know every single word in the sentence. It also helped me to see various ways in which the vocabulary we learned in class were implemented; I think it helped me to reinforce words and phrases that I had previously learned.

5. Do you enjoy ER activities? Why or why not?
I enjoy the ER activities because it is fun to do something different every week, especially because it often gets us to do things in different groups. It is also fun to hear about the different stories that other people in the class have read.

6. What suggestions do you have for implementing ER in future classes?
I think it would be good to have more books so that there is more variety to choose from. I also think it would be good to have more activities that relate more directly to the content of the stories.

Figure 4 End-of-the-semester ER reflection.

Level 2 (450 Chinese characters). Publishers in the mainland of China have also published many graded readers for learners of Chinese as well as for native Chinese-speaking children (Table 6).

Points to Ponder
- Which ER activities do you find more engaging: traditional ones like book reports or creative ones such as *The Story and Drawing*? Why?

4.3 Spanish

A few ER studies in learning Spanish as a foreign or second language contexts have been conducted (e.g., Hardy, 2013, 2016; Liburd & Rodrigo, 2012). For example, Hardy (2016) documented the effects of a short-term

Table 6 Chinese graded readers published in the Chinese mainland.

Graded readers	Publisher	Year of publication	# of levels
《七色龙汉语分级阅读》 Rainbow Dragon Graded Chinese Readers	Foreign Language Teaching and Research Press	2018	3
《我的中文小书包》 * My Little Schoolbag Leveled Chinese Readers	Foreign Language Teaching and Research Press	2021	6
《小羊上山儿童汉语分级读物》 * Little Sheep Goes Up the Mountain: A Graded Chinese Reader for Children	Posts & Telecom Press	2022	5
《"彩虹桥"汉语分级读物》 Rainbow Bridge Graded Chinese Reader	Sinolingua	2015	7
《学汉语分级读物》 Graded Readers for Chinese Language Learners	Beijing Language and Culture University Press	2014	3
《中文小书架—汉语分级读物》 The Chinese Library Series – Chinese Graded Readers	Beijing Language and Culture University Press	2014	4
《凤烈鸟——汉语分级绘本》 * Phoenibird—Chinese Picture Books	Beijing Language and Culture University Press	2019	3

Title	Publisher	Year	
《留学生汉语分级阅读指南》 Graded Chinese Reading Guide for International Students	Beijing Language and Culture University Press	2017	5
《好朋友——汉语分级读物（青少版）》 Friends—Chinese Graded Readers (for Teenagers)	Beijing Language and Culture University Press	2014	6
《好朋友——汉语分级读物（成人版）》 Friends—Chinese Graded Readers (for Adults)	Beijing Language and Culture University Press	2014	6
《实用汉语分级阅读丛书》 Practical Chinese Graded Reading Series	Beijing Language and Culture University Press	2008	4
《手拉手》 Hand in Hand	Foreign Language Teaching and Research Press	2021	2
《你真棒》 You're Awesome	Foreign Language Teaching and Research Press	2021	4
《汉语风》 中文分级系列读物 Chinese Breeze:Chinese Graded Readers	Peking University Press	2011	4
《轻松猫中文分级读物》 Smart Cat Graded Chinese Readers	Beijing Language and Culture University Press	2016	4
《一点悦读儿童中文分级读物》 * A Little Joy Reading Children's Chinese Graded Reader	China Zhigong Press	2021	4

Table 6 (cont.)

Graded readers	Publisher	Year of publication	# of levels
迪士尼《宝宝自己读 (1–4级)》* Baby Reading by Himself (Grades 1–4)	Posts & Telecom Press	2010	4
迪士尼《我会自己读》* I can Read by Myself	Posts & Telecom Press	2016	8
《小小语言家汉语分级阅读》* Little Linguist: Graded Chinese Readers	Liaoning Children's Publishing House	2019	5
《一亩宝盒分级阅读绘本》* One Acre of Treasure Box Graded Reading Picture Book	China Welfare Institute Publishing House Juvenile & Children's Publishing House	2019	6
《一阅而起汉语分级阅读绘本 (1–6级)》* Leap into Chinese Graded Reading	The Open University of China Press	2022	6
《芝麻开花汉语分级阅读》* Graded Chinese Reading Picture Book (Levels 1–6)	Language & Culture Press	2021	3
《汉字子集儿童汉语分级绘本》* Subset of Chinese Characters: Graded Chinese Picture Book for Children	Sichuan Children's Publishing House	2022	1
《我会读》* I Can Read	China People's Publishing House	2011	2
《宝宝自己会读》* Babies Can Read on Their Own	Qingdao Publishing House	2015	6
《小马宝莉大声朗读故事》* My Little Pony	Foreign Language Teaching and Research Press	2017	4

《少儿汉语阶梯读物》 Diving into Chinese	Higher Education Press	2015	4
《华语阅读金字塔》 Sinolingua Reading Tree	Sinolingua	2018	13
《中文天天读》 Reading China	Foreign Language Teaching and Research Press	2011	5
《小小语言家·汉语分级读物》* Little Linguist:Graded Readers	Liaoning Children's Publishing House	2023	3

Note. * indictates graded readers written for native-speaking Chinese children.

In conclusion, the practice of ER in the context of L2 Chinese is still in its early stages. There is a growing need for further research.

extensive reading program on Spanish proficiency, motivation to read, and
attitudes toward reading in Spanish in a mixed-ability class. The study was
conducted in a small, private, liberal arts college in the United States. ER
was offered as a stand-alone elective course in which students at the intermediate through low-advanced levels were encouraged to enroll. The course
met three hours per week for seven weeks. Most of the class time was
devoted to students' silent sustained reading. The reading materials were
graded readers, adapted classics, and children and young adult books in
Spanish collected by the researcher's department. Students were also able to
check out children's, young adult, and adult literature books from a local
public library. Data were collected through cloze tests, a Spanish language
proficiency test (i.e., Brigham Young University's Computer Adaptive
Placement Test), a questionnaire, and reflection journals. Students also
kept a reading log to record the date, the title of the book, the number of
pages read, the number of minutes read, and an indication of the difficulty
level of the book. The results of a cloze test showed a significant improvement in Spanish proficiency after seven weeks of ER. The reflective journals
showed that ER offered opportunities for them to guess the meaning of
unknown words using contextual clues. Students also found out that reading
in Spanish became easier and more enjoyable. Most students identified
improvements in their reading comprehension in Spanish, and many identified improvements in their vocabulary, reading fluency, and even writing
and speaking abilities in Spanish. For example, the following are some
quotes from students' reflection journals (p. 58):

Quote 1:
I have started to be more comfortable with the process of reading in
Spanish. The time that I have spent reading in this class has helped me to
think in Spanish when I'm reading . . . . . .

Quote 2:
My reading ability in Spanish has developed a lot in the past weeks . . . .
I can read in Spanish without looking for words that I don't know and still
understand the book. This class is very beneficial.

Quote 3:
. . . I have seen that now I'm reading much more fluently. I'm also writing
much better in Spanish. This class has opened my eyes to which it really is to
read.

The study provided insightful implications for incorporating ER into L2 Spanish
curriculum. The study underscored the importance of having an ample selection of
books that are interesting and easy. When graded readers are unavailable,

instructors can turn to children's or young adult's literature in a local public library, as Hardy did. Instructors' guidance toward selecting appropriate book levels was also needed on the students' side. Hardy (2016) called for the inclusion of ER in the Spanish as a foreign language curriculum.

Liburd and Rodrigo (2012) investigated the effects of a five-week short-term ER program on reading attitudes and confidence of L2 Spanish learners enrolled in a second-semester Spanish class at a university in the Southeastern United States. Around 100 graded Spanish readers and 48 books at pre-Level 1 were available. At the end of the five weeks, each participant in the ER group ($n = 3$) read a total of 5 books for an average of 169 pages each. Among the fifteen books students selected to read, eleven were from Level 1, two from pre-Level 1, and two from Level 2. Both the ER group and the traditional group reported identical L1 reading attitude and pre-L2 reading attitude. However, the post-L2 reading attitude of the ER group improved by 1.33 while that of the control group showed no change in their attitude scores. ER also played a role in boosting confidence in the reading ability of the experimental group. The students in the ER group also supported the inclusion of ER into the Spanish curriculum. Liburd and Rodrigo's (2012) study demonstrated the feasibility of incorporating ER as a supplement to L2 Spanish courses. They stated that reading a book per week is a manageable task that can be done along with the regular course curriculum. Particularly, it showed how ER could be incorporated into a lower-level L2 Spanish course as a supplement component. The results of the study, however, need to be interpreted with caution due to the very small sample size in both the control and experimental groups.

Points to Ponder
- Please choose a Spanish graded reader and design one post-reading activity.

4.4 German

Same as L2 Spanish, there are only a few published studies that reported the incorporation of ER into German language programs (e.g., Arnold, 2009; Rankin, 2005). The two studies reported the implementation of ER among intermediate-level learners (Rankin, 2005) and advanced-level learners (Arnold, 2009), thus providing implications for doing ER with learners of different proficiency levels.

Rankin (2005) reported on the incorporation of ER into an intermediate German course at Princeton University. The course where ER was incorporated was German 102-5, an honors section of Intermediate German. Students were highly motivated and had higher expectations for the course. The reading materials for the course were a combination of short stories and internet texts. After consultation with students and taking other factors into consideration, it was decided that ER would be done after class, for a minimum of one to two hours per week. There was also no requirement on the number of books read, rather, it would be the time involved that counted. Students were asked to turn in book reports, briefly explaining the texts read and providing an evaluation. The reading materials used included the *Easy Reader* series from Klett Verlag and texts in Langenscheidt's series of *Leichte Lekütren* (p. 128). Readers can refer to Rankin (Appendix A) for a list of graded readers in L2 German. Data were collected using reading report sheets, an anonymous survey at the end of the semester, and a formal interview with some students. The researcher was interested in students' perceptions of ER materials. Students reported that ER materials gave them a sense of empowerment and enjoyment in the act of L2 reading. For example, here is one quote from one student:

> I always looked forward to doing the extensive reading because it was so enjoyable to be able to read in German without having to look up every other word. Though the stories were of course not so intellectually challenging as the "real" texts we read. I neither expected or wanted them to be. (p.130)

Some respondents responded that ER helped with their German grammar, a greater comprehension of the German language, and lexis. What also appealed to the participants was that ER allowed them to read at their own pace and there were no tests. However, at the same time, students suggested that ER could be more structured (e.g., add vocabulary quizzes, more frequent book reports, and write book journals) and assign a reading amount each week (e.g., one book a week). Rankin (2005) concluded that ER, if properly organized, can succeed in creating a positive attitude in learners toward the learning of German that transcends "a grade-mongering" and "a learn-for-the-test" mentality (p. 131).

Arnold (2009) evaluated the effects of ER among a group of advanced learners of German as a foreign language. ER was implemented in an advanced composition and conversation class. Each class lasted seventy-five minutes and students met twice per week. Over the course of the semester, seven ER sessions were conducted in computer labs. The instructor introduced a list of German websites (i.e., newspapers, magazines, news and radio stations, blogs, and others) to the students (see p. 364 Appendix A in Arnold, 2009). Students were encouraged to read what interested them without using a dictionary. Students read for the majority of the time in seventy-five minutes each class and then were asked to fill in a reading report before engaging in a follow-up reading discussion. The reading reports were part of a reading portfolio which was worth 30 percent of students' final grade. The reading reports were graded using a rubric that evaluated whether students analyzed the reading materials in terms of their content, genre, formality level, purpose, reflected on their reading processes, documented their reading strategies, and so on. The reading reports and questionnaire data showed that students read authentic texts on a wide range of topics that matched their interests. Almost 62 percent of students reported that they enjoyed reading the online materials in ER sessions. Students also used dictionaries, but mainly after reading. They realized the disruptive nature of dictionary use and were more comfortable reading without knowing each word. All students reported being more confident in their ability to read German and felt that they had become better readers in German. Overall, students were enthusiastic about selecting reading materials by themselves. One student (Laura) commented, "half the fun is in choosing" (p. 358). This accorded with Principle #3 *Learners choose what they want to read* of the top ten ER principles of Day and Bamford (2002). It seemed that students were able to select reading materials they felt comfortable reading and understand on average 84 percent of what they read. An interesting finding from Arnold (2009) was that five out of eight participants purposely chose more difficult texts to challenge themselves. This accorded with advanced learners in Tabata-Sandom (2023) where they gained a sense of achievement from reading challenging high-level readers on Xreading.com. As Arnold stated, those advanced learners made "conscious decisions" about a text's difficulty level and challenged themselves on purpose (p. 359). Arnold's approach was particularly valuable for upper-division language courses with students of heterogeneous proficiency levels and diverse needs.

Points to Ponder
- Identify reading materials suitable for ER in L2 German. Describe your selection criteria, and specify the learner group (e.g., beginners, intermediate, advanced) for whom you believe these materials are most appropriate, and explain your reasoning.

4.5 Japanese

A few ER studies have been conducted in Japanese as a foreign language (JFL) or Japanese as a second language (JSL) context (e.g., Hitosugi & Day, 2004; Leung, 2002; Suzuki & Kumada, 2018; Tabata-Sandom et al., 2023).

Leung (2002) examined the impact of ER on Wendy's (pseudo name) self-study of Japanese over a twenty-week period. Wendy lived in Hongkong for twenty years. Chinese was her first language and English was her second language. She was pursuing her master's degree in ESL (now Second Language Studies) at the University of Hawai'i at Manoa. The study was conducted in two stages, covering nine and eleven weeks respectively. By the end of the study, Wendy read thiry-two books, mainly comic books and children's books. Wendy kept diaries, recording her experience and the progress of reading Japanese. Occasionally, she also talked to her EFL professor about her progress and concerns about her learning Japanese through emails or after-class discussions. In the second stage, Wendy was also able to find a Japanese friend who helped her with her Japanese study for half an hour to one hour each week. Results of a modified Paribakht and Wesche's vocabulary test showed that Wendy's vocabulary knowledge increased by 23.5 percent in one month. The journal entries showed that ER reinforced her existing knowledge of certain vocabulary items and allowed her to apply her vocabulary knowledge in a meaningful way. Since Wendy was reading children's and comic books, she also learned some expressions that would not be normally found in textbooks. Wendy was also able to guess the meanings of unknown words and learned words incidentally. The following journal entry showed how she figured out the meaning of a word through multiple encounters in different contexts (Leung, 2002, p. 73, Journal entry, Week 16).

Wendy also improved her reading comprehension of Japanese. She had a hard time decoding *hiragana* at the beginning, At the end of the study, she was able to understand simple Japanese children's stories. Wendy's attitude to reading also fluctuated. In the beginning, she was excited, then she was frustrated because she could not find reading materials appropriate for her level. As her reading proficiency improved, she became more confident. She was also more tolerant of the complexity of the language and more motivated to improve her reading proficiency.

As could be expected, Wendy encountered some challenges in her self-ER reading, such as the difficulty of finding appropriate reading materials and time to read. Wendy, nevertheless, actively overcame those issues. She not only checked out books from a local library, but also turned to Japanese friends for advice, especially those with young children in the family. The implication of Wendy's experience is that if appropriate reading materials are available, it is possible that a beginning foreign language learner can practice ER and can "reap the benefits" (p. 79).

Hitosugi and Day (2004) elaborately reported the establishment of an ER program in a JFL context, the requirements of the program, the assessment of the reading, and students' perceptions. An ER component was incorporated into Jpn 102, a first-year, second-semester Japanese course at the University of Hawai'i at Manoa. Hitosugi and Day (2004, p. 23) stated that in order to add ER to Jpn 102, they need to address six key issues:

1. What would the students read?
2. Would the reading be required, with credit awarded, or would students simply be encouraged to read on an optional basis for the benefits it would have on their language learning?
3. How much reading would the students be required to do?
4. Would ER be done for homework, in class, or both?
5. How could we incorporate the students' reading into the course?
6. How could we measure the impact, if any, of reading extensively on the students' learning of Japanese?

Those key issues revolved around different aspects of ER as a teaching approach, including materials, the role of ER in the curriculum, reading amount, the format of ER, and assessment.

As for the reading materials, they collected 266 used and new books and classified them into 6 levels based on Hitosugi (2000) and with reference to proficiency levels of ACTFL. The number of books for each level was Level 1 (39), Level 2 (76), Level 3 (50), Level 4 (87), Level 5 (11), and Level 6 (3). The researchers also color-coded the levels so that students could easily select books. They assigned 10 percent of the final course grade to ER, thus making ER a required part of the course. This is different from some studies (e.g., Liburd & Rodrigo, 2012) where ER was a voluntary task.

As for the reading amount or *reading target*, as Hitosugi and Day named it (p. 26), students were required to read forty books over a ten-week period, which means four books a week. If students read over forty books, a 5 percent bonus credit would be awarded for reading an additional twenty books. Different from Zhou and Day (2023) where students read Chinese books both in and outside of the class, Hitosugi and Day decided to assign ER as part of homework to make sure that students keep up with those in the other eleven Jpn sections, which is also a practical issue to consider when one course has multiple sections. However, every week approximately thirty minutes of the class time were allocated to ER activities. For example, students may be asked to promote their favorite books, act out the story, or create sentences using vocabulary from the story. According to Hitosugi and Day (2004), classroom activities "validated" their ER (p. 27), strengthened the class as a "language-learning community" (p. 27), and served as an incentive for the students to do reading after class. I feel that Hitosugi and Day (2004) provided very clear and step-by-step guidance of how to establish an ER program in L2 Japanese contexts. Also conducted at the University of Hawai'i at Manoa, Mohar's study (2024) examined the implementation of ER among beginning Japanese learners in a university in the USA, the study revealed that beginning Japanese learners prefer graded readers over children's books and physical books over online materials, which provided pedagogical implications for material selection among beginning-level L2 Japanese readers.

While Hitosugi and Day's study was conducted in a JFL context, Tabata-Sandom et al. (2023) carried out a study on extensive reading (ER) in L2 Japanese within Japan. Their study involved eleven upper-intermediate to advanced-level undergraduate and graduate students studying Japanese at a national university in western Japan, who were enrolled in an elective ER course titled "Learning Japanese through ER." This course spanned two consecutive semesters, totaling sixteen weeks. The reading materials included 130 Japanese graded readers, comic books, books intended for native children, and books targeting native readers. Students were encouraged to engage in reading both in and outside the classroom, with those reading forty books achieving full marks. On average, each participant read 36.7 books per term. Echoing the findings of Hitosugi and Day (2004), this study also noted individual differences in the number of books read, with the most avid readers completing 140 books over the two terms and the least active reader finishing only 44 books. Unlike other ER studies in the L2 Japanese context, Tabata-Sandom et al. (2023) explored the impact of ten speed reading training sessions on the participants' reading rate. The results indicated a significant increase in reading speed across three different measurement methods, without compromising comprehension. Consequently, Tabata-Sandom et al. (2023) advocated for the integration of a speed-reading component into ER programs.

> **Points to Ponder**
> - What are the potential benefits and challenges of using Japanese manga as reading materials in L2 Japanese ER programs?
> - What are the potential benefits and challenges of using manga as reading materials in ER programs of other foreign languages?

4.6 French

There are not many published studies on ER in French as a foreign or second language. Besides Pigada and Schmitt (2006), which examined the learning of French words through extensive reading (please see 3.2 Vocabulary), I was able to find one master's thesis written in French. Jourdan-Ôtsuka (2022) conducted an ER study at the Kyoto University of Foreign Studies to examine the effectiveness of ER (LEx, which stands for Lecture Extensive) in French as a foreign language among 100 native Japanese students. This research, situated within the French Studies Department, primarily involved students who began their

French language learning journey at the university. Most had only previously studied English in their primary and secondary education. The objective of the students was to elevate their French proficiency from A2 to B1 level within a four-year timeframe.

The study used a diverse range of materials, primarily short and highly illustrated books, including children's picture books and online resources. These books were strategically chosen and classified based on word count to align with the students' varying proficiency levels. The 100 participants on average read 17 books. Participation in the LEx program was incorporated as a part of the curriculum, substituting a written comprehension exam and contributing to 25% of the final grade. Remarkably, 96% of the participants met the reading targets set by the program. To gauge the students' language proficiency and motivation, the Test de Connaissance du Français (TCF) online and end-of-semester surveys were utilized. The surveys also provided insights into the students' perceptions of the LEx program and their general reading habits.

The study revealed that L1 Japanese students learning French as a foreign language reported an increased interest in reading and a deeper appreciation of Francophone cultures. The study also revealed that learners in the more organized programs tended to perform better in the number of books read, average length of the books read, and total number of words read.

Points to Ponder
- Identify reading materials suitable for ER in L2 French. Describe your selection criteria, and specify the learner group (e.g., beginners, intermediate, advanced) for whom you believe these materials are most appropriate.

4.7 Italian

Adopting a longitudinal pre-post design, Aliyar and Peters (2022) investigated the effects of reading comic books on incidental vocabulary learning in an L2 Italian context. The participants were thirty-five Iranian learners of Italian as a foreign language with a mean age of 20.5 years old. Around 25 of the participants in the experimental group read and then read while listening to four comic books in a four-week period. The four comic books used in the study were *Una Storia Italiana, Il Mistero di Casanova, Rigoletto,* and *Habemus Papam*. Three aspects of vocabulary knowledge (i.e., form recall, meaning recall, and form recognition) of eighty-two Italian words that appeared in the comic books were selected as target words. Concerning the form recall format, students were asked to translate Persian words into Italian words. As for the meaning recall, the participants were asked to translate Italian target words to Persian. For the form recall test, the authors asked the participants to indicate the level of familiarity with each target word by choosing between three options (1. I have never seen this word before; 2. I have seen this word, but I don't know its meaning; 3. I know the meaning of this word.). The results showed that vocabulary could be learned incidentally through reading and reading while listening without explicit instruction. The qualitative data showed that most students loved learning Italian by reading comic books because the experience was pleasurable. They also stated that they would continue reading comic books in the future. Aliyar and Peters (2022) suggested that comics are a valuable and effective source of learning Italian, and their inclusion in L2 Italian teaching and learning can be particularly advantageous to L2 learners, especially those with elementary Italian proficiency.

Points to Ponder
- Aliyar and Peters (2022) identified comic books as reading materials suitable for elementary-level L2 Italian learners. Could you please identify reading materials suitable for intermediate and advanced-level learners and explain your reasoning?

5 ER across Contexts

5.1 Rural Settings

Language educators might be extremely interested in implementing ER in rural schools where reading might be the only language input for learners. Mohd Asraf and Ahmad (2003) introduced their experience of implementing an ER program, which they called the Guided Extensive Reading program, among a group of Malaysian rural school students. The students were from the 7th and 9th grades at three schools. The majority of the students from the three schools hardly speak English at home or school. Some of them spoke Malay at home, while some students spoke a Chinese dialect at home. The parents of the majority of the students were farmers or factory workers. Since the students had a very limited vocabulary in English, they read books at several levels below their actual grade level. One day of a week was assigned to ER where students read silently and then retell what they have read to their classmates. Teachers helped the students with difficult vocabulary. Data were collected through classroom observations, in-depth interviews with both teachers and students, and teacher diaries. Initial observation showed students did not read English books regularly and did not enjoy reading in

English. As a result, they had difficulty understanding the stories they read and looked up the meanings of words in dictionaries often although they were advised not to do so. Students also had difficulty retelling the stories in the first ER sessions. As a result, some of them merely copied texts from the stories and read them out. As the semester progressed, students were more motivated to read in English, felt that ER was beneficial to them, and grew to like reading English books. As Mohd Asraf and Ahmad (2003) concluded, students in rural schools could and did benefit from ER. The majority of the students developed positive attitudes toward reading in English. Further research is needed on ER in rural settings, where there may be a scarcity of reading materials and students might possess lower language proficiency levels compared to their peers in urban schools.

Points to Ponder
- What are some challenges of implementing ER in low-resource areas? How to overcome those challenges?

5.2 Advanced Learners

Advanced learners are, according to Tabata-Sandom (2023), "an under-researched population" in ER (p.160). In the ER field, learners are categorized as advanced either by their vocabulary size (i.e., Tabata-Sandom, 2023), by the level of courses being taken (e.g., an advanced composition and conversation class in Arnold, 2009), or by the results of certain types of proficiency tests (e.g., EAP students who took an English proficiency test in Zhou & Day, 2021).

Tabata-Sandom (2023) labeled the participants as advanced learners based on the average of their vocabulary sizes of 7,081 word families. The eleven participants aged between thirty and sixty-five whose L1 was Japanese were recruited via Facebook groups and a local book club and read graded readers on an online reading website for one year. On average, the 11 participants read 1,146,821 words over a year. The researcher found that many participants in her study completely embraced graded readers due to their comprehensibility. Through reading a large number of materials, the participants' vocabulary size increased significantly, with a medium effect size of $d = 1.04$. The participants' reading rate also increased from 123.8 SWPM to 153.2 SWPM. Overall, the study revealed that advanced L2 readers transformed from unconfident readers to engaged and avid L2 readers. Tabata-Sandom (2023) identified *comprehensible and intriguing reading materials, soft enforcement* (a sense of commitment to the ER project and consistent support from the researcher), *high L2 reading abilities,* and *positive reading attitudes* as the sources behind the change. Tabata-Sandom (2023) demonstrated how to start an ER program among mature adult learners with high L2 proficiency levels who are no longer enrolled in any language courses. Tabata-Sandom's (2023) study shed light on the role played by ER in L2 language geragogy (i.e., the education of older individuals).

Instead of using graded readers as in Tabata-Sandom (2023), another ER study with advanced learners introduced a list of German websites (i.e., newspapers, magazines, news and radio stations, blogs, and others) to the students in a German as a Foreign Language context (Arnold, 2009). Students appreciated the learner autonomy in material selection and held positive views of ER.

The implementation of ER with advanced language learners may encompass several key considerations: Firstly, it is essential to take the learners' proficiency levels into account during the preparation of materials and design of activities. Secondly, granting learners autonomy in the selection of reading materials, in particular challenging but intriguing materials, can be highly beneficial. Despite their higher language proficiency, advanced learners may experience reluctance or anxiety while reading in a foreign language, as noted in Tabata-Sandom's (2023) study. Therefore, it is both advisable and beneficial to encourage advanced learners to read extensively.

> **Points to Ponder**
> • Do you think advanced learners would benefit from ER? Why or why not?

5.3 EAP Contexts

Fifteen years ago, Macalister (2008) claimed that ER appeared to be particularly absent in higher educational and EAP settings. Fifteen years later, it would be safe to say that ER has gained popularity in universities, but I am afraid what Macalister said about ER in EAP settings still holds true today. There are only a few ER studies conducted in EAP contexts (e.g., Kim & Ro, 2023; Macalister, 2008; Park, 2016; Ro, 2018). However, ER can be a valuable teaching and learning approach in EAP contexts.

Macalister (2008) incorporated ER in a twelve-week university preparation EAP course in New Zealand. The course was designed to prepare students for university study. Students read silently for twenty minutes (sustained silent reading) at the end of each morning, with the teacher also "modelling good reading behavior" by reading silently with students (p. 250). Students were encouraged to read on their own time and as much as possible but were required to read at least two graded readers per week. The reading materials could be borrowed from the university's language learning center. Overall, the inclusion of ER as a component in the EAP course was positively perceived by the learners and to some extent created positive attitudes toward reading. Macalister (2008) was confident that ER can definitely "have a place" in EAP classrooms (p. 255).

Integrating reading and writing through ER, as Park (2016) argued, could be a valuable approach to help EAP learners deal more easily with the enormous amount of reading and writing in academic settings. University students expressed negative attitudes such as fear, anxiety, and stress toward academic reading in English (Eriksson, 2023) and integrating reading and writing is a challenge faced by EAP students (Grabe & Zhang, 2013). Comprehensible input provided by ER may have led to a pleasurable and less demanding writing experience, which in turn may have enhanced learners' writing fluency and facilitated L2 writing development.

Park (2016) explored the role of ER in L2 writing ability in an EAP program. Fifty-six participants were from two writing classes, a traditional one and an ER-oriented one. Students in the ER-oriented writing class spent fifteen minutes reading graded readers and five minutes discussing their reading in pairs or groups, while students in the traditional writing class spent fifteen minutes on free writing, followed by five minutes of pair discussion. ER group borrowed books from the ER library which contained around 250 books of both fiction and nonfiction (e.g., biography and history). The graded readers were mainly from *Oxford Bookworms* by Oxford University Press and *Cambridge English Readers* by Cambridge University Press. Both classes were also required to spend around one and a half hours on homework per week. While the traditional writing class participants were given textbook-based homework each week (e.g., writing short essays, grammar exercises), the ER-oriented class participants were asked to continue ER and complete a writing activity based on the books they read to practice writing skills such as summarizing, describing, analyzing, creative writing and so on. To measure the writing ability, essay tests with the prompt "What is your attitude towards writing?" were administered at the beginning and the end of the semester. The results showed that the ER class outperformed the traditional class in five sub-skills of writing: *content, organization, vocabulary, language use,* and *mechanics*. It seemed that ER helped students learn how to use words and expressions in appropriate contexts and produced more natural-sounding sentences (Park, 2016).

Through continuous encounters with grammatical expressions, students may have learned new grammar knowledge or strengthened their existing knowledge of English grammar, such as subject–verb agreement, singular/plural nouns, prepositions, articles, and so on (Park, 2016). Similarly, Kim and Ro (2023) also showed that an ER group significantly improved in *the length of sentences, the number of clauses*, and *the number of verb phrases* compared to students in a control group. ER group also used *frequent verbs* and *verb construction combinations* to a lesser extent.

Zhou and Day (2021) investigated whether reading self-selected easy books could improve academic reading and different aspects of language abilities in EAP settings. Fifty-seven undergraduate and graduate EAP learners participated in the ER program. The students were from two EAP courses: intermediate and advanced academic reading courses. Both EAP reading courses met for seventy-five minutes, twice a week, for sixteen weeks. Online ER was required and implemented in both courses. The number of words required to read differed in two instruction levels: 10,000 words per week for the intermediate EAP reading course and 13,000 for the advanced EAP reading course in the Fall 2017 semester (reduced to 12,000 for the Spring 2018 semester). Students were asked to read online from Xreading.com each week and take online quizzes with 60% accuracy. Around 10% of the course grade was assigned to ER in both courses. The study collected both quantitative data (i.e., pre- and post-reading attitude questionnaires, students' online reading records), and instructors' and students' interviews. Overall, 57 EAP learners spent 14 hours reading extensively online and read 18 books and 91,077 words in one semester. As for whether ER improved their academic reading, 45 percent of the interviewees agreed that ER improved their academic reading ability. The interview data showed that ER made them *feel confident and comfortable* in reading, which further *motivated students to read academic materials like textbooks*.

Besides having a direct impact on EAP reading ability, ER may also indirectly influence EAP reading ability through the mediation of affective factors such as *confidence or comfort*. This is especially important in EAP contexts because academic reading tasks such as reading research articles and textbooks, summarizing, and writing literature reviews, and so on are often daunting tasks. Gaining confidence and feeling comfort in reading graded materials may make EAP students get used to reading. Confidence in one's reading ability is an important affective variable in creating independent readers (Liburd & Rodrigo, 2012). Excerpt 1 from Zhou and Day (2021) demonstrated how ER impacted academic reading ability. Excerpt 2 is a suggestion from one interviewee.

Excerpt 1

> Z: Ok, great, so do you think reading those self-selected books improve your academic reading?
>
> L: Yeah, I think so.
>
> Z: Oh, how?
>
> L: I think before I don't like reading but I became to like reading, so before I hesitate to read my textbook, but now I can read much faster than before.
>
> Z: So you want to read?
>
> L: Yeah. Actually.
>
> Z: So you think Xreading helps?
>
> L: Yeah, very helps.

There is no denying that graded readers and research articles or textbooks differ in many ways. Some interviewees did not agree that ER contributed to their academic reading ability. Two reasons EAP students mentioned included: (1) reading materials are not on academic topics and (2) students did not select to read academic books (Zhou & Day, 2021). One interviewee said that ER and academic reading are not related. One instructor also mentioned that there were complaints from students that many books on Xreading are for children and "childish." One suggestion, as stated in Excerpt 3, might be that teachers play a bigger role in material preparation. This accords with one suggestion in Teng's (2023) discussion piece of Zhou and Day (2021).

Excerpt 2

> Z: Good, do you agree that reading self-selected easy books help improve your academic reading?
>
> P2: Uh uh, it did help improve my academic reading, but *I won't recommend it to be always self-selected to students.*
>
> Z: Oh
>
> P2: *Sometimes you like have to give them a challenge, give them something to read, not something that they want to read.*
>
> . . . . . .
>
> P2: Yeah, ... I would also recommend that they should read the articles from newspapers, or something like that, you know, so they can have a better in-depth of reading.

Teachers can enrich the ER experience in EAP contexts by diversifying the reading materials. This can include newspapers, magazines, online resources (e.g, Arnold, 2009), and academic texts. It is important to tailor these materials to EAP learners' individual interests, their proficiency levels, and their specific academic objectives. Additionally, language instructors should offer ongoing guidance and support to EAP learners. Providing personalized scaffolding is crucial for the effective implementation of ER in EAP settings.

Points to Ponder
- How can ER programs be tailored to address the specific reading and writing demands faced by EAP learners?
- Given the mixed perceptions of ER's impact on academic reading abilities among EAP students, what role should instructors play in ER programs to ensure both engagement and academic relevance for EAP learners?

5.4 Online ER

With the development of technology over the recent decades, using online information to read is an integral part of our lives. Reading has transformed from printed papers to a variety of digital texts. The new trend has dramatically changed the direction of ER and offered opportunities for language teachers to incorporate online ER into their course syllabus (Bui & Macalister, 2021). The advantages of ebooks over physical books have also been supported in previous research (e.g., Cote & Milliner, 2015; Jeon & Day, 2016). Recent five years have witnessed many online ER studies (e.g., Bui & Macalister, 2021; Perez, 2022; Puripunyavanich, 2022; Rezaee et al., 2021; Tabata-Sandom, 2023; Zhou & Day, 2021). Online ER studies refer to studies that use online reading materials, such as graded readers, newspapers, magazines, video clips, and so on.

Puripunyavanich (2022) implemented an online ER program among 5,000 freshmen at a university in Thailand. An online ER reading platform, Xreading .com, was used because it suited the large-scale implementation of ER in that university with ease of access, the ability to track and monitor the reading progress, and a variety of reading materials at different levels (Puripunyavanich, 2022). The study attributed the success of the ER program to five factors, including *the integration of ER into the curriculum, the availability of reading materials, the institution's support, teachers' roles,* and *the use of an online platform.* Zhou and Day (2021) and Tabata-Sandom (2023) also adopted Xreading.com because it enabled learners and researchers in both studies to monitor individual reading progress closely. Rezaee et al (2021) showed that some Iranian EFL learners preferred working with multimedia texts (e.g., video clips, audio files, pictures, hyperlinks) over physical books. Cost is another factor influencing the choice of e-materials over physical books (e.g., Cote & Milliner, 2015; Puripunyavanich,

2022). Electronic materials can be offered at lower costs compared to physical books (Cote & Milliner, 2015).

Some instructors also developed their own online ER platforms to meet specific reading needs of their students. For example, Bui and Macalister (2021) developed a reading website called Extensive Reading Online (ERO) on wordpress.com for seventeen EFL learners at a university in Vietnam. The reading materials in this small-scale digital library were adapted and collected from a number of online resources such as *English ER Central, gradedreading .com, Lit2Go, Paul Nation's website, World Stories UK,* and *365 ESL short stories* (p. 6). In order to provide the most natural reading experience, the website only integrated two functions: a stopwatch to enable students to record their reading time and an online progress graph for them to keep track of their reading progress.

With the help of my institution's IT department, I developed an online ER website *IChineseER* (https://lchineseer.sites.pomona.edu) for L2 Chinese learners. The website provides over 300 graded reading materials on topics related to Chinese culture such as holidays, Chinese food, ethnic groups, idioms, and jokes. The materials were categorized into 6 levels (A1 = 4; A2 = 84; B1 = 52; B2 = 83; C1 = 53; C2 = 5) with reference to the Common European Framework of Reference for Languages (CEFR).

L1 Japanese EFL learners in Li et al. (2023) read on BookRoll ebook reader, a teaching resource distribution system designed to access ebooks and lecture slides. BookRoll ebook reader provided 400 ebooks. Students can navigate the reading content page by page, make markers in yellow or red, create memos, or search keywords in an ebook. More importantly, students' reading behaviors can be recorded and stored for research or teaching purposes. Thus, with some help from IT experts, language teachers can establish online reading platforms that cater to learners' needs in specific contexts.

In conclusion, the evolution of technology and the transition to digital media have significantly influenced the implementation of ER. Online ER platforms not only facilitate the tracking and monitoring of reading progress but also integrate multimedia elements to enrich the learning experience, underscoring the significant opportunities that online ER brings to the teaching and learning of reading.

Points to Ponder
- What opportunities and challenges do online materials bring to foreign language readers?
- What functionalities should be prioritized in the development of online ER platforms to support and motivate language learners at different proficiency levels?

6 Implementing ER

6.1 Challenges

Despite the beneficial merits of ER, it is still a less commonly adopted approach to language teaching (e.g., Chang & Renandya, 2017; Ewert, 2020; Renandya & Jacobs, 2002; Robb & Ewert, 2024) and the ER approach "has not become more popular" (Robb, 2022, p. 184). As Jeon and Day (2016) observed, ER is yet not widely practiced in language classrooms, particularly in EFL settings (Jeon & Day, 2016). Bui and Macalister (2021) stated that the implementation of ER seems to be limited in many higher education classrooms due to teachers' time commitment (Grabe, 2001) and the skeptical view of language educators. Alahirsh (2014) identified the main obstacles to implementing an ER program as limited time allocated for reading, the cost associated with purchasing reading materials, and challenges in managing a program. A peruse of the literature (Chang & Renandya, 2017; Grabe, 2011; Haider, 2012; Huang, 2015; Macalister, 2010; Renandya & Jacobs, 2002; Renandya et al., 2020; Renandya et al., 2021; Robb, 2022) reveals a list of challenges pertaining to students, teachers, curriculum, materials, and so on.

Reflective break
• Why do you think ER is not widely adopted?

6.1.1 Students

Some students simply do not like reading, even in their L1. Some students enjoy reading in their L1, but reading in L2 is a daunting task (e.g., advanced L2 learners in Tabata-Sandom, 2023). This might be due to previous negative reading experience or low language proficiency, or they are simply not used to reading in their L2, or have never attempted to read a large amount of materials in an L2 (e.g., Robb & Ewert, 2024). As a result, some L2 learners dislike reading and don't read. For example, Mikami (2017) surveyed 141 Japanese EFL learners about their reading experience in English. Only 5 of 141 students (3.55 percent) regularly read English books other than their course textbooks. Reasons for negative desire to read extensively in English included *difficulty, lack of ability, no interest, low priority, preference for native language, lack of confidence, lack of opportunity,* and *no need* (Mikami, 2017). Teachers in the Asian context in Chang and Renandya (2017) reported difficulties in implementing ER. Two of the top reasons were *students not being interested in reading* and *students having difficulty reading independently.* Adhikari and Shrestha (2023) showed that *students' poor reading habits* and *students' increased use of social media* prevented students from reading extensively.

> **Points to Ponder**
> • As a foreign language learner, do you enjoy reading in your foreign language (s)? Why or why not?

6.1.2 Teachers

Teachers encountered many challenges while implementing ER (e.g., Al Aghar et al., 2023; Chang & Renandya, 2017; Fan, 2023; Habib & Watkins, 2023; Stewart, 2014).

Firstly, language teachers may not be equipped with theories and/or practices of ER or have a misunderstanding of the nature of ER (e.g., Arai, 2019; Fan, 2023; Wang & Kim, 2021). For example, using both quantitative questionnaires and qualitative interviews, Fan (2023) investigated the attitudes and understanding of ER among a group of Chinese EFL professors. It showed that the professors looked down upon simplified texts and viewed ER as a means for linguistic study, not for pleasure, general understanding, or information. Thus, ER was perceived as intensive reading done by students independently. Similarly, Arai (2019) revealed that a group of Japanese EFL pre-service teachers either had a misunderstanding of the nature of ER or were not fully aware of the benefits of ER. Chinese EFL teachers described themselves as "blind" if without proper training for ER (Sun, 2020, p. 218). Some language teachers did not have experience of extensive reading in the target language. As a result, they teach as how they were taught (Robb, 2022).

Secondly, teachers may have difficulty monitoring students' reading. For example, teachers face difficulties identifying if students are reading efficiently and thoroughly (e.g., Stewart, 2014). Chang and Renandya (2017) reported that teachers had difficulty in monitoring students' reading and difficulty in assessing students' learning for reading.

Thirdly, if ER was done online, some teachers may encounter technical difficulties. For example, EAP teachers in Zhou and Day (2021) stated that they encountered technical issues.

Fourth, many language curriculums have fixed schedules, so it might be hard for language teachers to find time for ER. When curriculum completion is the focus of language classrooms, teachers would have difficulty finding additional time for integrating ER into the classroom (Habib & Watkins, 2023).

What has been mentioned so far are only a few challenges teachers may encounter in implementing ER.

> **Points to Ponder**
> • In the context where you currently teach or plan to teach, what challenges might you encounter when establishing an ER program, and how could you address these challenges?

6.1.3 Institutions

Institutional-level factors should also be taken into account when designing an ER program. When administrators or stakeholders are fully aware of the benefits of ER, it is possible for a large-scale ER to be implemented in the curriculum. For example, language teachers mentioned *curriculum having a fixed schedule* as one of the challenges in implementing ER (Chang & Renandya, 2017). *An unsupportive institutional environment* was also listed in Adhikari and Shrestha (2023) as a reason preventing ER from being conducted. The reason why stakeholders have reservations about ER might be related to the legitimacy of ER (Renandya et al., 2015). Students doing sustained silent reading in class may not be perceived as a legitimate classroom learning activity (Prowse, 2002). Institutions might also opt to discontinue ER programs due to feedback from teachers or students. For example, Flanagan and Custance (2017) reported that a school in western Japan ended an ER program, which had been in operation for several years because teachers reported no noticeable improvement in students' reading abilities.

> **Points to Ponder**
> • As a language teacher, what strategies would you use to demonstrate the value of ER to school administrators?

6.1.4 Materials

Previous research (Macalister, 2015; Robb, 2022) pointed out that graded reading materials, the main form of reading materials for ER programs, are not available in many countries around the world or are too expensive for local schools to afford. Intriguing reading materials are essential to ER programs. Principle #2 of the top ten ER principles (*A variety of reading material on a wide range of topics is available*) was followed by thirty-five out of forty-four ER programs according to Day (2015). However, extensive reading materials and graded readers were not available in some countries or regions (e.g., in Ethiopia, Endris, 2018; the situation may have changed after 2018). Since there are not many reading materials available, "freedom of choice" of reading materials is also not realistic (Robb, 2022, p. 187). Moreover, different publishers utilize varied-level systems, which can complicate the process for language teachers when selecting materials. For instance, an analysis of 203 Spanish-language graded readers from 12 publishers uncovered no unified criteria for assessing reading difficulty levels (Rodrigo, 2016). These inconsistencies present significant challenges for selecting materials efficiently.

Points to Ponder
• How can ER program coordinators navigate the issue of limited availability and high cost of graded readers in certain regions?

6.2 Strategies

6.2.1 Incorporating ER in the Language Curriculum

Jeon and Day (2016) highlighted the ease of implementing ER when it is integrated into the school curriculum. This sentiment is further reinforced by Habib and Watkins (2023), who stated that: "the only way to legitimize extensive reading is to establish it as a part of the curriculum and assessment" (p.52). Language teachers, administrators, and policymakers can be convinced of ER's credibility and its myriad benefits in language learning. Chang and Renandya (2017) suggested that incorporating ER into the language curriculum enables teachers to allocate curriculum time for student reading.

A practical example of this implementation is seen in Robb and Kano's (2013) study, where the school administration mandated the integration of ER across the entire nonmajor English language course curriculum. Macalister (2010) emphasized the importance of this approach, stating: "Clearly, school managers, administrators, and even possibly principals need to be aware of the reasons for incorporating extensive reading into the teaching program. This may be particularly important in situations where teachers feel that their teaching program is severely constrained by an imposed syllabus." (p. 71).

In conclusion, the integration of ER into the language curriculum is not only feasible but essential for legitimizing ER. With institutional support and curriculum adjustments, ER can significantly benefit learners across various educational contexts.

Points to Ponder
- Considering the specific context in which you currently teach (e.g., educational level, geographical location), what are the potential barriers to incorporating ER into the foreign language curriculum, and how might these be overcome?

6.2.2 Materials

The availability of intriguing and diverse reading materials is a key to the success of an ER program. Day and Bamford (1998) proposed that a variety of materials could be used in ER programs, including but not limited to children's books, graded readers, cartons, newspapers, websites, posts, blogs, series readers, and so on.

Previous ER studies have also reported the adoption of different kinds of materials in ER programs, such as graded readers (Abdulrahman & Kara, 2023; Robb & Kano, 2013), websites (e.g, Arnold, 2009), L1 children's literature (e.g., Macalister & Webb, 2019), original novels (e.g., McQuillan, 2020; Sun, 2020), manga comics (Anggraini, 2014), and series readers (i.e, books by the same authors, Renandya et al., 2018). In L2 English, a vast array of ER materials is available. According to Thomas Robb, Chair of the Extensive Reading Foundation (T. Robb, personal communication, February 26, 2024), Mreader's master list comprises 13,040 L2 English readers, of which 6,249 are graded readers and 6,791 are categorized as youth literature (i.e., anything other than graded readers). Notably, there are more nongraded readers than graded ones. These nongraded readers primarily consist of "leveled readers" designed for native-speaking children (T. Robb, personal communication, February 26, 2024). The Extensive Reading Foundation website also has information on the number of graded readers in languages other than English (Extensive Reading Foundation, n.d., https://erfoundation.org/wordpress/grs-in-other-languages/). Language teachers who are interested in implementing ER but lack graded readers can turn to L1 children's literature, which is relatively abundant in number (e.g., graded readers for L1 Chinese children in Table 6 – 4.2 Chinese). Japanese manga, a type of "non-traditional material"[1], is also an appealing ER material

---

[1] One of the reviewers named mangas as "non-traditional materials."

and is available in languages such as French, Spanish, Italian, German, Korean, and Chinese.

In terms of the mode of reading, there is a growing trend of ER conducted online (e.g., Bui & Macalister, 2021; Puripunyavanich, 2022; Tabata-Sandom, 2023; Zhou & Day, 2023), using online reading websites such as Xreading.com (https://xreading.com) (see also 5.4 Online ER). Online ER websites are introduced in published studies (e.g., readtheory.com in Robb & Ewert, 2024) or in published website reviews (e.g., Ponddy Reader, Zhou & Zhao, 2023; Newsela, Nushi & Fadaei, 2020; L2 reading website, Alzahrani, 2022; Xreading.com, Wilkins, 2019).

Some language teachers, being themselves technical experts or collaborating with technology experts, IT departments, or other departments in their institutions, developed online reading platforms. A few examples include *BookRoll* for EFL learners (Li et al., 2023), *IChineseER* for L2 Chinese readers (https://lchineseer.sites.pomona.edu) by me, and *Extensive Reading Online* by Bui and Macalister (2021).

As for the selection of materials, the common practice is to allow language learners to make the selection. But when a variety of materials is not available, teachers can also select materials for students. Recent research has also shown that students read both teacher-selected and student-selected materials (e.g., Chen, 2018; Sun, 2020). Chinese secondary school EFL learners trusted teachers' choice and enjoyed teacher-selected materials (e.g., Sun, 2020). In Chen (2018), the first stage of ER involved the whole class reading teacher-selected material while in the second stage, students read self-selected texts.

ER materials and activities can also be incorporated into textbooks. Textbooks can be a powerful and effective medium for promoting ER (Brown, 2009), which can provide credibility and legitimacy to the ER approach (Renandya et al., 2015). Some textbook writers incorporated ER principles while writing textbooks. For example, Renandya et al. (2015) reviewed eight ER textbooks for both English majors and non-English majors used in universities in China and found that three out of the eight textbooks received fairly high scores based on nine evaluation principles (e.g., The coursebook provides interesting and comprehensible reading materials; The coursebook contains tasks and activities designed to help develop students' fluency in reading) (pp. 259–261). Thus, it seems that some textbook writers are aware of the key features of ER and made "a deliberate attempt to include these features in the design of their coursebooks" (p. 271). *Kernel Lessons Intermediate* edited by O'Neill et al. (1971) included a continuous story "The Man Who Escaped" for extensive reading.

Cover to Cover edited by Day and Harsch (2008) contained excerpts from graded readers to encourage learners to engage in ER.

Points to Ponder
- Considering the diverse ER materials available, how might this diversity impact learner motivation and engagement?

6.2.3 Teacher Training

An important step before incorporating ER into a language curriculum is to make sure that language teachers are in accord with the nature of ER, the theories underlying ER, the principles of ER, the selection of ER materials, the designing of ER activities, the monitoring of students' reading, and the benefits of ER. This can be achieved through systematic reading of existing ER literature, attending ER conferences (e.g., Extensive Reading World Congress), exchanging with colleagues who also implement ER, and so on. Elturki and Harmon (2020, p. 5) listed the following professional development activities:

- reading and discussing literature on ER
- attending training or virtual seminars on ER (e.g., Extensive Reading and Language Learning by Dr. Richard Day offered through the TESOL International Association)
- establishing a working group of instructors to assess how the reading curriculum and instruction are done in the program (e.g., Is it intensive reading–heavy? How can intensive reading and ER be balanced?)
- conducting a workshop in which all instructors come together to brainstorm possible ways to conduct ER and locate resources
- creating opportunities for faculty peer observations to explore different pedagogical applications of ER

Glen Hill (2014) posted a list of basic variables related to ER program implementation on ExtensiveReading@yahoogroups.com. Those questions can be used in teacher training to inspire thinking and discussion among teachers.

- are classes required or not?
- how many books are available, and at what levels and in how many copies per book?
- is the reading itself done in the classroom/library, only outside class time, or both?
- what do teachers expect from students after they read a book? (Moodle comprehension quiz, short comment, book report, etc.)

- how does a student move up in levels, and how were they placed into a starting level?
- what activities, if any, are done in class to follow up on silent reading? (discussion, drawing, letter writing to author, etc.)
- how is the concept of ER introduced to students, and in what language?
- how does the teacher actually encourage students during the semester, especially when they aren't doing what they should? (May 9, 2014)

Points to Ponder
- What are some professional development opportunities available for language teachers interested in implementing ER?

6.2.4 ER Orientation

L2 readers will be more inclined to participate in ER if they understand its benefits. Rahmawati's (2018) study revealed that students believed they would enjoy ER more if they "knew what to read, how to read, and why they read" (p. 130). Being aware of the benefits of ER is essential to change learners' attitudes toward ER (Habib and Watkins, 2023). This Element as well as abundant previous research (e.g., meta-analyses research) has summarized and introduced the linguistic and affective benefits of ER. As has been stated, ER contributes to reading fluency, enhances vocabulary and grammar knowledge, promotes a positive reading attitude and reading motivation, and helps with the formation of good reading habits. ER also makes readers more confident and comfortable in reading. As a result, they experience flow and achieve an optimal reading experience. Thus, ER programs need to provide well-designed orientation to students. A clear and comprehensive introduction to the definition of ER, the principles of ER, the benefits of ER, the reading goals, and the reading materials is advised to be conducted.

Points to Ponder
- Why is an orientation important for language teachers and learners?
- What should be covered in an ER orientation?

6.2.5 Setting Clear Goals

The critical role of motivation in shaping and sustaining reading habits underscores the importance of establishing clear reading goals in ER programs.

Research by Fujii (2022), Li et al. (2021), and Leather and Uden (2021) has emphasized the significance of thoughtful goal-setting in ER, particularly regarding the number of books to be read, which is especially beneficial for readers at lower proficiency levels (as noted by de Lozier, 2019). Additionally, leveraging external motivators, such as course credits or awards, can serve as an initial impetus for students to embark on their reading journey, as described by Habib and Watkins (2023, p. 50). An example of this can be seen in a Japanese EFL program, where setting specific word targets (e.g., 2,500 words per week) led to extrinsic motivation, eventually fostering intrinsic motivation among learners (McLean & Poulshock, 2018). Moreover, studies have shown that commitment to these goals can positively affect intrinsic motivation and self-efficacy. Achieving goals can create a positive feedback loop, enhancing student motivation and engagement in ER, as evidenced in Mikami's research (2017, 2020).

> **Points to Ponder**
> - How do you think setting specific reading goals (e.g., number of books, word targets) influences the motivation and reading habits of learners?

6.2.6 Teachers' Guidance and Support

The role of the teacher is pivotal in the successful implementation of ER programs. As identified in the literature, teachers in ER programs fulfill diverse roles including being role models (Day & Bamford, 2002), program managers and reading advisors (Yamashita, 2013), as well as motivators and monitors (Sze, 1999) (refer to Habib & Watkins, 2023 for further insights). Their support and guidance are particularly crucial in ensuring ER's meaningful impact, especially for beginner learners.

Research has highlighted various methods through which teachers or researchers can facilitate students' reading. In a study by Mohd Asraf and Ahmad (2003), teachers and researchers provided direct support in Malaysian rural schools by clarifying unknown vocabulary in the classroom. Tabata-Sandom (2023) extended emotional support to participants through regular, personalized emails and weekly newsletters over a year, recommending books and sharing reviews, along with individualized comments on reading progress (e.g., "You've reached 500,000 words! Awesome!") (p.166). Zhou and Day (2023) engaged with students by reviewing book reports, correcting language errors, and offering affirmative feedback like "好" (Well done!). Further, language teachers can monitor students' reading progress through activities such as writing book reports, taking quizzes (for instance, using Mreader as in

Mitchell, 2019, and Al Damen, 2018), or participating in ER-related activities (Bamford & Day, 2004).

In conclusion, teachers can significantly aid students by involving them in post-ER activities (Zhou & Day, 2023), providing vocabulary scaffolding (Taguchi et al., 2004), and maintaining interpersonal communication via emails and news-letters (Tabata-Sandom, 2023). It is essential for teachers to support students who may feel overwhelmed, thereby boosting their confidence in reading (Mikami, 2017). I concur with Lenand et al. (2022) that teachers can ignite a passion for reading among learners and cultivate enthusiastic and lifelong readers.

Points to Ponder
- Reflect on the unique role of an ER teacher in fostering students' reading development. As a creative exercise, please think of a metaphor to describe an ER teacher.
- An ER teacher is _____.

7 Epilogue: The Potential of ER

Establishing ER programs demands time, commitment, careful planning, and passion. While initiating an ER program might not be overly challenging, ensuring its sustainability over the years can be a more complex endeavor. As Macalister (2010) insightfully observed, "any extensive reading program is going to be affected by a range of factors and so the program must be flexible in order to suit the particular learners" (p. 31).

A wealth of research supports ER's effectiveness in enhancing the teaching and learning of reading, leading to the emergence of several new trends. One such trend is the increasing focus on the cognition and beliefs of ER teachers. For instance, Conaway and Parsons (2023) investigated how a group of EFL teachers set reading targets in ER classes and their underlying rationales.

Another burgeoning trend is providing learners with multimodal materials. Abdulrahman and Kara (2023) had students read graded readers like *The Adventures of Tom Sawyer*, *Lord of the Flies*, and *Forrest Gump*, followed by watching the respective movie adaptations. This was complemented by discussions in a campus café, where students explored the main themes of the movies and engaged in various novel-related questions. Additionally, practices like reading while listening have gained positive reception in ER programs (Isozaki, 2018; Tragant Mestres et al., 2019).

Furthermore, ER is increasingly being integrated with other reading approaches such as speed reading, timed reading, and repeated reading (Holsworth, 2020; Shimono, 2023; Tabata-Sandom et al., 2023; Tusmagambet, 2020). It is also being combined with diverse teaching and learning approaches including task-based language teaching (Chen, 2018), extensive listening (Tsuda et al., 2023), cooperative learning (Tsuda et al., 2023), project-based learning (Singh et al., 2022), and reading strategies training (Shih et al., 2018) to amplify ER's benefits.

In conclusion, the evolving landscape of ER research demonstrates its dynamic and adaptable nature. By embracing new trends and methodologies, ER continues to evolve, offering enriched, multifaceted learning experiences. These developments not only enhance the appeal of ER but also ensure its relevance and efficacy in the ever-changing realm of language education.

References

Abdulrahman, S. A., & Kara, S. (2023). The effects of movie-enriched extensive reading on TOEFL IBT vocabulary expansion and TOEFL IBT speaking section score. *Journal of Qualitative Research in Education*, *33*, 176–197. https://doi.org/10.14689/enad.33.913.

Adhikari, B. R., & Shrestha, K. N. (2023). Extensive reading at the university level: Why is it trivialized in practice? *Journal of NELTA Gandaki*, *6*(1–2), 1–12. https://nelta.org.np/nelta/uploads/web-uploadsfiles/English%20Journal.pdf.

Aka, N. (2019). Reading performance of Japanese high school learners following a one-year extensive reading program. *Reading in a Foreign Language*, *31*(1), 1–18. https://nflrc.hawaii.edu/rfl/item/414.

Aka, N. (2020). Incidental learning of a grammatical feature from reading by Japanese learners of English as a foreign language. *System*, *91*, 102250. https://doi.org/10.1016/j.system.2020.102250.

Al Aghar, T., Demirci, H. C., Houjeir, R., McMinn, M., & Alzaabi, K. A. S. (2023). Investigating Arabic teachers perceptions of extensive reading practices in higher education. *Cogent Education*, *10*(1), 2162701. https://doi.org/10.1080/2331186X.2022.2162701.

Al Damen, T. M. (2018, August). The effectiveness of M-reader in promoting extensive reading among Arab EFL Learners. *Arab World English Journal (AWEJ) Proceedings of 1st MEC TESOL Conference*. https://dx.doi/10.24093/awej/MEC1.1.

Alahirsh, H. (2014). *Exploring the effectiveness of extensive reading on incidental vocabulary acquisition by EFL learners: An experimental case study in a Libyan university* [Doctoral dissertation, University of Nottingham].

Alexander, J. E., & Filler, R. C. (1976). *Attitudes and reading*. International Reading Association.

Aliyar, M., & Peters, E. (2022). Incidental acquisition of Italian words from comic books. *Reading in a Foreign Language*, *34*(2), 349–377. http://hdl.handle.net/10125/67429.

Alzahrani, R. (2022). Review of L2 reading websites. *Reading in a Foreign Language*, *34*(1), 195–203. http://hdl.handle.net/10125/67420.

Anggraini, P. (2014). Manga comics as appealing extensive reading materials for the tenth graders of senior high school. The 61 TEFLIN International Conference, UNS Solo 2014 [Proceedings]. 343–346. https://core.ac.uk/reader/43025510.

Arai, Y. (2019). Extensive reading definitions, effectiveness, and issues concerning practice in the EFL classroom: Japanese teacher trainees' perceptions. *Journal of Extensive Reading, 7*, 15–32.

Arai, Y. (2022). Perceived book difficulty and pleasure experiences as flow in extensive reading. *Reading in a Foreign Language, 34*(1), 1–23. http://hdl.handle.net/10125/67410.

Arnold, N. (2009). Online extensive reading for advanced foreign language learners: An evaluation study. *Foreign Language Annals, 42*(2), 340–366. https://doi.org/10.1111/j.1944-9720.2009.01024.x.

Bala, A. (2022). The attitudes of EFL Students towards extensive reading program in digital library in private primary school (A case of Erbil). *International Journal of Social Sciences & Educational Studies, 9*(1), 383–392. https://doi.org/10.23918/ijsses.v9i1p383.

Bamford, J., & Day, R. R. (2004). *Extensive reading activities for teaching foreign language*. Cambridge University Press.

Beglar, D., & Hunt, A. (2014). Pleasure reading and reading rate gains. *Reading in a Foreign Language, 26*(1), 29–48. http://hdl.handle.net/10125/66684.

Beglar, D., Hunt, A., & Kite, Y. (2012). The effect of pleasure reading on Japanese university EFL learners' reading rates. *Language Learning, 62*(3), 665–703. https://doi.org/10.1111/j.1467-9922.2011.00651.x.

Bell, T. (2001). Extensive reading: Speed and comprehension. *The Reading Matrix, 1*(1), 1–13.

Birketveit, A., Rimmereide, H. E., Bader, M., & Fisher, L. (2018). Extensive reading in primary school EFL. *Acta Didactica Norge, 12*(2), 1–23. https://doi.org/10.17863/CAM.32342.

Boutorwick, T. J., Macalister, J., & Elgort, I. (2019). Two approaches to extensive reading and their effects on l2 vocabulary development. *Reading in a Foreign Language, 31*(2), 150–172. http://hdl.handle.net/10125/66928.

Brown, D. (2009). Why and how textbooks should encourage extensive reading. *ELT Journal, 63*(3), 238–245.

Brysbaert, M. (2019). How many words do we read per minute? A review and meta-analysis of reading rate. *Journal of Memory and Language, 109*, 104047. https://doi.org/10.1016/j.jml.2019.104047.

Bui, T., & Macalister, J. (2021). Online extensive reading in an EFL context: Investigating reading fluency and perceptions. *Reading in a Foreign Language, 33*(1), 1–29. http://hdl.handle.net/10125/67391.

Carrel, P. L., & Carson, J. G. (1997). Extensive and intensive reading in an EAP setting. *English for Specific Purposes, 16*, 47–60. https://doi.org/10.1016/S0889-4906(96)00031-2.

Chan, V. (2020). To read or not to read: A critical evaluation of the effectiveness of extensive reading in ESL/EFL contexts. *Social Sciences and Education Research Review, 7*(2), 48–68.

Chang, A. C., & Renandya, W. A. (2017). Current practice of extensive reading in Asia: Teachers' perceptions. *The Reading Matrix: An International Online Journal, 17*(1), 40–58.

Chen, I. C. (2018). Incorporating task-based learning in an extensive reading programme. *ELT Journal, 72*(4), 405–414. https://doi-org.ccl.idm.oclc.org/10.1093/elt/ccy008.

Cohen, J. (1988). *Statistical power analysis for the behavioral sciences* (2nd ed.). Lawrence Erlbaum.

Conaway, P., & Parsons, A. (2023). ER and reading targets: An investigation into teachers' choices and their rationales. *Journal of Extensive Reading, 10* (3), 1–23.

Cote, T., & Milliner, B. (2015). Implementing and managing online exensive reading: Student performance and perceptions. *IALLT Journal of Language Learning Technologies, 45*(1), 70–90.

Csikszentmihalyi, M. (1988). The flow experience and its significance for human psychology. In M. Csikszentmihalyi, & I. Csikszentmihalyi (Eds.), *Optimal experience: Psychological studies of flow in consciousness* (pp. 15–35). Cambridge University Press.

Csikszentmihalyi, M., Abuhamdeh, S., & Nakamura, J. (2005). Flow. In A. J. Elliot, & C. S. Dweck (Eds.), *Handbook of competence and motivation* (pp. 598–608). The Guilford Press.

Daskalovska, N. (2018). Extensive reading and vocabulary acquisition. In R. Ponniah, & S. Venkatesan (Eds.), *The idea and practice of reading* (pp. 25–40). Springer. https://doi.org/10.1007/978-981-10-8572-7_3.

Day, R., & Bamford, J. (1998). *Extensive reading in the second language classroom.* Cambridge University Press.

Day, R., & Bamford, J. (2002). Top ten principles for teaching extensive reading. *Reading in a Foreign Language, 14*(2), 136–141. http://hdl.handle.net/10125/66761.

Day, R. R. (2013). *Teaching reading.* TESOL International Association.

Day, R. R. (2015). Extending extensive reading. *Reading in a Foreign Language, 27*(2), 294–301. http://hdl.handle.net/10125/66893.

Day, R. R., & Harsch, K. (2008). *Cover to cover: Book 2.* Oxford University Press.

Day, R. R., & Swan, J. (1998). Incidental learning of foreign language spelling through targeted reading. *TESL Reporter, 31*, 1–9.

de Burgh-Hirabe, R., & Feryok, A. (2013). A model of motivation for extensive reading in Japanese as a foreign language. *Reading in a Foreign Language*, *25*(1), 72–93. http://hdl.handle.net/10125/66678.

de Lozier, C. D. (2019). Motivation, proficiency and performance in extensive reading. *International Journal of Innovation and Research in Educational Science*, *6*(3), 442–453.

Demirci, H. C. (2019). *Extensive reading in the English as a second language classroom – motivating and engaging male Emirati students in a higher education context* [Unpublished dissertation, The University of Liverpool].

Elturki, E., & Harmon, E. (2020). Systematic integration of extensive reading in the curriculum: Strategies and resources. *TESOL Journal*, *11*(3), e00517. https://doi.org/10.1002/tesj.517.

Endris, A. A. (2018). Effects of extensive reading on EFL learners' reading comprehension and attitudes. *International Journal of Research in English Education*, *3*(4), 1–11. https://ijreeonline.com/article-1-113-en.html.

Engeser, S., & Shiepe-Tiska, A. (2012). Historical lines and an overview of current research on flow. In S. Engeser (Ed.), *Advances on flow research* (pp. 1–22). Springer.

Eriksson, L. (2023). Difficulties in academic reading for EFL students: An initial investigation. *Language Teaching*, *56*(1), 149–152. https://doi.org/10.1017/S0261444822000246.

Ewert, D. (2020). ER for statistical learning. In M. Dressman, & R. Saddler (Eds.), *Wiley handbook on informal learning* (pp. 395–404). Wiley.

Extensive Reading Foundation. (n.d.). *GRs in other languages*. Retrieved February 28, 2024, from https://erfoundation.org/wordpress/grs-in-other-languages/.

Fan, H. (2023). Talking past each other: Chinese EFL teachers' understanding of extensive reading. *Journal of Extensive Reading*, *10*(4).

Flanagan, A., & Custance, I. M. (2017). The rise and fall of an extensive reading program. *Extensive Reading in Japan (ERJ)*, *10*(2), 10–14. http://jalt.org/er/sites/jalt.org.er/files/ERJ/erj_issue_10.2.pdf.

Fongpaiboon, A. (2017). *A study of extensive reading and flow experience among EFL Thai university students* [Doctoral dissertation, Thammasat University]. http://grad. litu. tu.ac.th/assets/public/kcfinder/upload_grad_web/public/5_2017_ARIYADHORN%20FONGPAIBOON_4-6-18.pdf.

Fujii, K. (2022). The effects of a two-year-long extensive reading program on TOEIC Bridge IP scores. *The Reading Matrix: An International Online Journal*, *22*(2), 108–120.

Goodman, K. S. (2014). Reading: A psycholinguistic guessing game. In K. S. Goodman, & Y. M. Goodman (Eds.), *Making sense of learners making sense of written language* (pp. 103–112). Routledge.

Grabe, W. (2001). Reading-writing relations: Theoretical perspectives and instructional practices. In D. Belcher & A. Hirvela (Eds.), *Linking literacies: Perspectives on L2 reading-writing connections* (pp. 15–47). The University of Michigan Press.

Grabe, W. (2009). *Reading in a second language: Moving from theory to practice.* Cambridge University Press.

Grabe, W. (2010). Fluency in reading – thirty-five years later. *Reading in a Foreign Language, 22,* 71–83. http://hdl.handle.net/10125/66645.

Grabe, W. (2011, September 5). Extensive reading: Why isn't everyone doing it? Plenary address at the First Extensive Reading World Congress. Final draft of notes. https://erfoundation.org/wordpress/wp-content/uploads/2022/02/Grabe-ERWC1 Plenary_Notes.pdf.

Grabe, W., & Zhang, C. (2013). Reading and writing together: A critical component of English for academic purposes teaching and learning. *TESOL Journal, 4*(1), 9–24. https://doi.org/10.1002/tesj.65.

Habib, F., & Watkins, P. (2023). Investigation of attitudes and barriers to extensive reading project in Saudi female English as a foreign language preparatory year program students and teachers. *The Reading Matrix: An International Online Journal, 23*(2), 47–66.

Haider, M. (2012). Extensive reading in EFL classroom at secondary schools in Bangladesh: Current practices and future possibilities. *International Education Studies, 5*(3), 126–133. https://doi.org/10.5539/ies.v5n3p126.

Hardy, J. E. (2013). *Extensive reading in Spanish as a foreign language and its effects on language proficiency, reading habits, motivation, and attitudes toward reading.* Paper presented at the Second Extensive Reading World Congress, Seoul, Korea.

Hardy, J. E. (2016). The effects of a short-term extensive reading course in Spanish. *Journal of Extensive Reading, 4*(3), 47–68. http://jalt-publications.org/jer/.

Hitosugi, C. (2000). Criteria for categorizing Japanese books. Unpublished manuscript.

Hitosugi, C. I., & Day, R. R. (2004). Extensive reading in Japanese. *Reading in a Foreign Language, 16*(1), 20–30. http://hdl.handle.net/10125/66593.

Holsworth, M. J. (2020). *The effect of extensive reading, timed reading, and word recognition training on reading* [Doctoral dissertation, Temple University].

Horst, M. (2005). Learning L2 vocabulary through extensive reading: A measurement study. *Canadian Modern Language Review, 61*(3), 355–382. https://doi.org/10.3138/cmlr.61.3.355.

Huang, Y.-C. (2015). Why don't they do it? A study on the implementation of extensive reading in Taiwan. *Cogent Education, 2*(1), 1099187. https://doi.org/10.1080/2331186X.2015.1099187.

Huffman, J. (2014). Reading rate gains during a one-semester extensive reading course. *Reading in a Foreign Language, 26*(2), 17–33. http://hdl.handle.net/10125/66879.

Isozaki, A. H. (2018). Reading-listening and reading circles: Bimodal approaches building fluency. *The Reading Matrix: An International Online Journal, 18*(1), 82–103.

Iwahori, Y. (2008). Developing reading fluency: A study of extensive reading in EFL. *Reading in a Foreign Language, 20*(1), 70–91. http://hdl.handle.net/10125/66626.

Iwata, A. (2022). The effectiveness of extensive reading (ER) on the development of EFL learners' sight vocabulary size and reading fluency. *The Reading Matrix: An International Online Journal, 22*(2), 74–91.

Jeon, E. H., & Yamashita, J. (2022). L2 reading comprehension and its correlates. In E. H. Jeon, & J. Yamashita (Eds.), *Understanding L2 proficiency: Theoretical and meta-analytic investigations* (pp. 29–86). John Benjamins.

Jeon, E. Y., & Day, R. R. (2016). The effectiveness of ER on reading proficiency: A meta-analysis. *Reading in a Foreign Language, 28*(2), 246–265. http://hdl.handle.net/10125/66901.

Jourdan-Ôtsuka, R. (2022). *La lecture extensive en français langue étrangère : Facteurs d'efficacité* (Extensive reading in French as a foreign language: Effectiveness factors) [Master's thesis, Université d'Angers].

Jun, H. (2018). *The gamification of extensive reading: Investigating the effects in L2 reading motivation, reading amount, and time spent reading* [Doctoral dissertation, Seoul National University].

Kim, H., & Ro, E. (2023). Additive extensive reading and syntactic development in second language writing: Analyses of syntactic complexity and sophistication in young EFL learners book reports. *Journal of Second Language Writing, 61*, 101040. https://doi.org/10.1016/j.jslw.2023.101040.

Kirchhoff, C. (2013). L2 extensive reading and flow: Clarifying the relationship. *Reading in a Foreign Language, 25*(2), 192–212. http://hdl.handle.net/10125/66867.

Kirchhoff, C., & Mision, M. (2022). Audio-assisted extensive reading: Learners' experience and attitudes. *The Reading Matrix: An International Online Journal, 22*(2), 1–12.

Klassen, K. , & Allan, T. (2019). Evaluating an extensive reading course. *Language Research Bulletin, 33*, 22–33. https://ci.nii.ac.jp/naid/120006650279/.

Klassen, K. , & Green, M. (2019). Comparing the effect of two extensive reading treatments on receptive vocabulary knowledge. *Language Research Bulletin, 34*, 17–25.

Kramer, B., & McLean, S. (2019). L2 reading rate and word length: The necessity of character-based measurement. *Reading in a Foreign Language, 31*(2), 201–225. https://nflrc.hawaii.edu/rfl/item/425.

Krashen, S. (1981). *Second language acquisition and second language learning*. Prentice Hall.

Krashen, S. D. (1992). The input hypothesis: An update. In A. E. James (Ed.), *Linguistics and language pedagogy: The state of the art* (pp. 409–431). Georgetown University Press.

Krashen, S. D. (2004). *The power of reading: Insights from the research*. Bloomsbury.

Krashen, S. D. (2009). The Goodman/Smith hypothesis, the input hypothesis, the comprehension hypothesis, and the (even stronger) case for free voluntary reading. In A. L. Patricia (Ed.), *Defying convention, inventing the future in literary research and practice* (pp. 46–60). Routledge.

Krulatz, A. M., & Duggan, J. (2018). Multilinguals and extensive reading: Two multilinguality portraits of learners of Norwegian. *Reading in a Foreign Language, 30*(1), 29–48. http://hdl.handle.net/10125/66737.

Kuperman, V., Siegelman, N., Schroeder, S., et al. (2023). Text reading in English as a second language: Evidence from the Multilingual Eye-Movements Corpus. *Studies in Second Language Acquisition, 45*(1), 3–37. https://doi.org/10.1017/S0272263121000954.

Leather, S., & Uden, J. (2021). *Extensive reading: The role of motivation*. Routledge.

Lee, J., & Schallert, D. L. (2016). Exploring the reading – writing connection: A yearlong classroom-based experimental study of middle school students developing literacy in a new language. *Reading Research Quarterly, 51*(2), 143–164. https://doi.org/10.1017/S0272263121000954.

Lee, J., Schallert, D. L., & Kim, E. (2015). Effects of extensive reading and translation activities on grammar knowledge and attitudes for EFL adolescents. *System, 52*, 38–50. https://doi.org/10.1016/j.system.2015.04.016.

Leland, C. H., Lewison, M., & Harste, J. C. (2022). *Teaching children's literature: It's critical!* (3rd ed.). Routledge. https://doi-org.ccl.idm.oclc.org/10.4324/9781003246947.

Leung, C. Y. (2002). Extensive reading and language learning: A diary study of a beginning learner of Japanese. *Reading in a Foreign Language, 14*(1), 66–81. http://hdl.handle.net/10125/66579.

Li, H., Majumdar, R., Chen, M. R. A., & Ogata, H. (2021). Goal-oriented active learning (GOAL) system to promote reading engagement, self-directed learning behavior, and motivation in extensive reading. *Computers & Education, 171*, 104239. https://doi.org/10.1016/j.compedu.2021.104239.

Li, H., Majumdar, R., Chen, M. R. A., Yang, Y., & Ogata, H. (2023). Analysis of self-directed learning ability, reading outcomes, and personalized planning behavior for self-directed extensive reading. *Interactive Learning Environments, 31*(6), 3613–3632. https://doi.org/10.1080/10494820.2021.1937660.

Liburd, T., & Rodrigo, V. (2012). The affective benefits of extensive reading in the Spanish curriculum: A 5-week case study. *The International Journal of Foreign Language Teaching, 7*(2), 16–20. https://ijflt.com/wpcontent/uploads/2021/03/IJFLT.Liburd.Rodrigo3.12.pdf.

Liu, H., & Chu, C. J. (2008). *Chinese breeze graded reader series*. Beijing University Press.

Liu, J., & Zhang, J. (2018). The effects of extensive reading on English vocabulary learning: A meta-analysis. *English Language Teaching, 11*(6), 1–15. http://doi.org/10.5539/elt.v11n6p1.

Lyddon, P. A. , & Kramer, B. (2019). Connecting extensive reading to TOEIC performance. In F. Meuiner, J. Van de Vyver, L. Bradley, & S. Thouësny (Eds.), *CALL and complexity – short papers from EUROCALL 2019* (pp. 257–262). Research-publishing.net. https://doi.org/10.14705/rpnet.2019.38.1019.

Macalister, J. (2008). Implementing extensive reading in an EAP programme. *ELT Journal, 62*(3), 248–256. https://doi.org/10.1093/elt/ccm021.

Macalister, J. (2010). Investigating teacher attitudes to extensive reading practices in higher education: Why isn't everyone doing it? *RELC Journal, 41*(1), 59–75. https://doi.org/10.1177%2F0033688210362609.

Macalister, J. (2015). Guidelines or commandments?: Reconsidering core principles in extensive reading. *Reading in a Foreign Language, 27*(1), 122–128. https://doi.org/10125/66703.

Macalister, J. & Webb, S., (2019). Can L1 children's literature be used in the English language classroom? High frequency words in writing for children. *Reading in a Foreign Language, 31*(1), 62–80. http://hdl.handle.net/10125/66750.

Maclauchlan, K. (2018). Bibliobattles in a university-level extensive reading classroom setting. *Extensive Reading Classrooms, 46*, 3–29.

McLean, S., & Poulshock, J. (2018). Increasing self-efficacy and reading amount in EFL learners with word targets. *Reading in a Foreign Language, 30*(1), 76–91. http://hdl.handle.net/10125/66739.

McQuillan, J. (2020). Harry Potter and the prisoners of vocabulary instruction: Acquiring academic language at Hogwarts. *Reading in a Foreign Language, 32*(2), 122–142. http://hdl.handle.net/10125/67377.

McQuillan, J. L. (2019). The inefficiency of vocabulary instruction. *International Electronic Journal of Elementary Education, 11*(4), 309–318. https://doi.org/10.26822/iejee.2019450789.

Mermelstein, A. D. (2015). Improving EFL Learners' writing through enhanced extensive reading. *Reading in a Foreign Language, 27*(2), 182–198. http://hdl.handle.net/10125/66890.

Mikami, A. (2017). Students' attitudes toward extensive reading in the Japanese EFL context. *TESOL Journal, 8*(2), 471–488. https://doi.org/10.1002/tesj.283.

Mikami, Y. (2017). Relationships between goal setting, intrinsic motivation, and self-efficacy in extensive reading. *JACET Journal, 61*, 41–56. https://doi.org/10.32234/jacetjournal.61.0_41.

Mikami, Y. (2020). Goal setting and learners' motivation for extensive reading: Forming a virtuous cycle. *Reading in a Foreign Language, 32*(1), 29–48. https://nflrc.hawaii.edu/rfl/item/438.

Mitchell, C. (2019). Preparing for extensive reading in an English communication course: An MReader solution. *PanSIG 2018 Journal*, 145–154.

Mohar, B. (2024). Can beginner JFL learners do ER?: Text comprehension, reading rate, materials, and reading targets for beginner JFL reading. Manuscript submitted for publication.

Mohd Asraf, R., & Ahmad, I. S. (2003). Promoting English language development and the reading habit among students in rural schools through the Guided Extensive Reading program. *Reading in a Foreign Language, 15*(2), 83–102. http://hdl.handle.net/10125/66772.

Mori, S. (2002). Redefining motivation to read in a foreign language. *Reading in a Foreign Language, 14*(2), 91–110. http://hdl.handle.net/10125/66765.

Mori, S. (2015). If you build it, they will come: From a "Field of Dreams" to a more realistic view of extensive reading in an EFL context. *Reading in a Foreign Language, 27*(1), 129–135. https://nflrc.hawaii.edu/rfl/item/319.

Nakamura, J., & Csikszentmihalyi, M. (2002). The concept of flow. In C. R. Snyder, & S. J. Lopez (Eds.), *Handbook of positive psychology* (pp. 89–105). Oxford University Press.

Nakamura, J., & Csikszentmihalyi, M. (2009). Flow theory and research. In S. J. Lopez, & C. R. Snyder (Eds.), *The Oxford handbook of positive psychology* (2nd ed.) (pp. 195–206). Oxford University Press.

Nakanishi, T. (2015). A meta-analysis of extensive reading research. *TESOL Quarterly, 49*, 6–37. http://doi.10.1002/tesq.157.

Nakano, T. (2023). Exploring the possibility of incidental grammar learning through extensive reading: Effectiveness of form-focused Japanese graded readers. *The Reading Matrix: An International Online Journal, 23*(2), 1–12.

Nassaji, H. (2014). The role and importance of lower-level processes in second language reading. *Language Teaching, 47*(1), 1–37. https://doi.org/10.1017/S0261444813000396.

Nation, I. S. P. (2001). *Learning vocabulary in another language.* Cambridge University Press.

Nation, I. S. P. (2006). How large a vocabulary is needed for reading and listening? (Version 1). Open Access Te Herenga Waka-Victoria University of Wellington. https://doi.org/10.26686/wgtn.12552221.v1.

Nation, I. S. P., & Heatley, A. (1996). *VocabProfile, word, and range: Programs for processing text.* Wellington: LALS, Victoria University of Wellington.

Nation, I. S. P., & Waring, R. (2019). *Teaching extensive reading in another language.* Routledge.

Ng, Q. R., Renandya, W. A., & Chong, M. Y. C. (2019). Extensive reading: Theory, research and implementation. *TEFLIN Journal, 30*(2), 171–186. https://doi.org/10.15639/teflinjournal.v30i2/171-186.

Nishino, T. (2007). Beginning to read extensively: A case study with Mako and Fumi. *Reading in a Foreign Language, 19*(2), 76–105.

Nishizawa, H., Yoshioka, T., & Nagaoka, M. (2018). How many words should elementary EFL learners read extensively and from which readability levels. *Journal of National Institute of Technology, Toyota College, 50*, 1–12.

Nushi, M., & Fadaei, M. H. (2020). Newsela: A level-adaptive app to improve reading ability. *Reading in a Foreign Language, 32*(2), 239–247. http://hdl.handle.net/10125/67381.

Nuttall, C. (1996). *Teaching reading skills in a foreign language.* Heinemann.

Odo, D. M. (2020). The impact of extensive reading and affective factors on achievement in the EFL writing classroom. *Teacher Education Research, 59*(3), 385–398.

O'Neill, R., Kingsbury, R., & Yeadon, T. (1971). *Kernel lessons intermediate.* Longman Group.

Park, A. (2020). A comparison of the impact of extensive and intensive reading approaches on the reading attitudes of secondary EFL learners. *Studies in Second Language Learning and Teaching, 10*, 337–358. https://doi.org/10.14746/ssllt.2020.10.2.6.

Park, A., Isaacs, T., & Woodfield, H. (2018). A comparison of the effects of extensive and intensive reading approaches on the vocabulary development of Korean secondary EFL learners. *Applied Linguistics Review, 9*(1), 113–134. https://doi:10.1515/applirev-2017-0025.

Park, J. (2016). Integrating reading and writing through extensive reading. *ELT Journal, 70*, 287–295. https://doi.org/10.1093/elt/ccv049.

Perez, M. M. (2022). Second or foreign language learning through watching audio-visual input and the role of on-screen text. *Language Teaching, 55*(2), 163–192. https://doi.org/10.1017/S0261444821000501.

Perfetti, C. (2007). Reading ability: Lexical quality to comprehension. *Scientific Studies of Reading, 11*(4), 357–383. https://doi.org/10.1080/108884307 01530730.

Perfetti, C. A. (1985). *Reading ability.* Oxford University Press.

Perfetti, C. A. (1992). The representation problem in reading acquisition. In P. B. Gough, L. C. Ehri, & R.Treiman (Eds.), *Reading acquisition* (pp. 145–174). Lawrence Erlbaum Associates.

Perfetti, C. A. (1999). Comprehending written language: A blueprint of the reader. In C. M. Brown, & P. Hagoort (Eds.), *The Neurocognition of Language* (pp. 167–208). Oxford University Press.

Pigada, M., & Schmitt, N. (2006). Vocabulary acquisition from extensive reading: A case study. *Reading in a Foreign Language, 18*(1), 1–28. http://hdl.handle.net/10125/66611.

Plonsky, L., & Oswald, F. L. (2014). How big is "big"? Interpreting effect sizes in L2 research. *Language Learning, 64*(4), 878–912. https://doi.org/10.1111/lang.12079.

Prowse, P. (2002). Top ten principles for teaching extensive reading: A response. *Reading in a Foreign Language, 14*(2), 142–145. http://hdl.handle.net/10125/66762.

Puripunyavanich, M. (2022). The implementation of a large-scale online extensive reading program in Thailand – from decision-making to application. *LEARN Journal: Language Education and Acquisition Research Network, 15* (1), 320–360.

Rahmawati, I. N. (2018). Extensive reading: A pilot project to change students' perception on reading. *Journal of Extensive Reading, 4*, 127–130.

Rankin, J. (2005). Easy reader: A case study of embedded extensive reading in intermediate German L2. *Die Unterrichtspraxis / Teaching German, 38*(2), 125–134. www.jstor.org/stable/20060000.

Renandya, W. A., Hu, G., & Xiang, Y. (2015). Extensive reading coursebooks in China. *RELC Journal, 46*(3), 255–273. https://doi.org/10.1177/00336882156 09216.

Renandya, W. A., Ivone, F. M., & Hidayati, M. (2021). Extensive reading: Top ten implementation issues. *JACET Journal, 65*, 11–21. https://willyrenandya .com/extensive-reading-top-tenimplementation-issues.

Renandya, W. A., & Jacobs, G. M. (2002). Extensive reading: Why aren't we all doing it? In J. C. Richards, & W. A. Renandya (Eds.), *Methodology in language teaching: An anthology of current practice* (pp. 295–302). Cambridge University Press.

Renandya, W. A., Krashen, S., & Jacobs, G. M. (2018). The potential of series books: How narrow reading leads to advanced L2 proficiency. *LEARN Journal: Language Education and Acquisition Research Network, 11*(2), 148–154. https://so04.tci-thaijo.org/index.php/LEARN/article/view/161631.

Rezaee, M., Farahian, M., & Mansooji, H. (2021). Promoting university students' receptive skills through extensive reading in multimedia-based instruction. *Journal of Applied Research in Higher Education, 13*(5), 1464–1489. https://doi.org/10.1108/JARHE-09-2020-0304.

Ro, E. (2013). A case study of extensive reading with an unmotivated L2 reader. *Reading in a Foreign Language, 25*(2), 213–233. http://hdl.handle.net/10125/66869.

Ro, E. (2018). Understanding reading motivation from EAP students' categorical work in a focus group. *TESOL Quarterly, 52*(4), 772–797. https://doi-org.ccl.idm.oclc.org/10.1002/tesq.426.

Robb, T. (2018). An introduction to online sites for extensive reading. *The Electronic Journal for English as a Second Language, 22*(1), 1–16.

Robb, T. (2022). Encouraging schools to adopt extensive reading: How do we get there? *Reading in a Foreign Language, 34*(1), 184–194. http://hdl.handle.net/10125/67419.

Robb, T. N., & Ewert, D. (2024). Classroom-based extensive reading: A review of recent research. *Language Teaching*, 1–30. https://doi.org/10.1017/S0261444823000319.

Robb, T. N., & Kano, M. (2013). Effective extensive reading outside the classroom: A large- scale experiment. *Reading in a Foreign Language, 25*(2), 234–247. http://hdl.handle.net/10125/66870.

Rodrigo, V. (2016). Graded readers: Validating reading levels across publishers. *Hispania, 99*(1), 66–86. www.jstor.org/stable/pdf/44112826.pdf.

Rodrigo, V., Greenberg, D., & Segal, D. (2014). Changes in reading habits by low literate adults through extensive reading. *Reading in a Foreign Language, 26*(1), 73–91. http://hdl.handle.net/10125/66688.

Sakurai, N. (2017). The relationship between the amount of extensive reading and the writing performance. *The Reading Matrix, 17*(2), 142–164.

Sakurai, N. (2023). Potential influence of extensive reading on controlled productive vocabulary. *Language Teaching Research*. https://doi.org/10.1177/13621688231171267.

Scales, A. M., & Rhee, O. (2001). Adult reading habits and patterns. *Reading Psychology, 22*(3), 175–203. https://doi.org/10.1080/027027101753170610.

Serrano, R. (2023). Extensive reading and science vocabulary learning in L2: Comparing reading-only and reading-while-listening. *Education Sciences, 13*(5), 493. https://doi.org/10.3390/educsci13050493.

Shen, H. H., & Ke, C. (2007). Radical awareness and word acquisition among nonnative learners of Chinese. *The Modern Language Journal, 91*(1), 97–111. https://doi.org/10.1111/j.1540-4781.2007.00511.x.

Shih, Y., Chern, C., & Reynolds, B. L. (2018). Bringing extensive reading and reading strategies into the Taiwanese junior college classroom. *Reading in a Foreign Language, 30*(1), 130–151. http://hdl.handle.net/10125/66742.

Shimono, T. R. (2023). The effects of extensive reading, timed reading, and repeated oral reading on Japanese university L2 English learners' reading rates and comprehension over one academic year. *Reading in a Foreign Language, 35*(2), 190–221. https://hdl.handle.net/10125/67447.

Singh, N. K. D., Jacobs, G. M., & Renandya, W. A. (2022). Integrating extensive reading with environmental education: A meaningful and engaging pedagogy approach. *Journal of English Language and Linguistics, 3*(2), 1–26.

Stewart, D. (2014). ER with online graded readers. *Extensive Reading in Japan, 7*(2), 16–18.

Stoeckel, T., McLean, S., & Nation, P. (2021). Limitations of size and levels tests of written receptive vocabulary knowledge. *Studies in Second Language Acquisition, 43*(1), 181–203. https://doi.org/10.1017/S027226312000025X.

Sun, X. (2020). An exploration of students and teachers perceptions of a two-year extensive reading program in a Chinese secondary school. *The Reading Matrix: An International Online Journal, 20*(1), 201–219.

Sun, Z., Yang, X. M., & He, K. K. (2016). An extensive reading strategy to promote online writing for elementary students in the 1: 1 digital classroom. *Computer Assisted Language Learning, 29*(2), 398–412. https://doi.org/10.1080/09588221.2014.974860.

Suzuki, M. , & Kumada, M. (2018). The role of extensive reading in Japanese as a second language. *CLaSIC 2018 Proceedings* (pp. 280–286). www.fas.nus.edu.sg/cls/CLaSIC/clasic2018/PROCEEDINGS/suzuki_mika.pdf.

Sze, V. Y. W. (1999). Promoting second language development and reading habits through an extensive reading scheme. In C. Y. Mee, & N. S. Moi (Eds.), *Language instructional issues in Asian classrooms* (pp. 69–84). International Development in Asia Committee.

Tabata-Sandom, M. (2023). A case study of the impact of online extensive reading on the L2 reading motivation, habits, and linguistic abilities of advanced L2 English learners. *Reading in a Foreign Language, 35*(2), 160–189. https://hdl.handle.net/10125/67446.

Tabata-Sandom, M., Banno, E., & Watanabe, T. (2023). The integrated effects of extensive reading and speed reading on L2 Japanese learners' reading fluency. *Journal of Extensive Reading, 10*(1), 1–24. https://jalt-publications .org/content/index.php/jer/issue/view/1206.

Taguchi, E., Takayasu-Maass, M., & Gorsuch, G. J. (2004). Developing reading fluency in EFL: How assisted repeated reading and extensive reading affect fluency development. *Reading in a Foreign Language, 16*(2), 70–96. http:// hdl.handle.net/10125/66783.

Takase, A. (2007). Japanese high school students' motivation for extensive l2 reading. *Reading in a Foreign Language, 19*(1), 1–18. http://hdl.handle.net/ 10125/66622.

Teng, M. F. (2023). Online extensive reading in EAP courses: Expanding on Zhou and Day's 2021 "online extensive reading in EAP courses." *Reading in a Foreign Language, 35*(2), 293–300. https://hdl.handle.net/10125/67451.

Tragant Mestres, E., Llanes Baró, À. , & Pinyana Garriga, À. (2019). Linguistic and non-linguistic outcomes of a reading-while-listening program for young learners of English. *Reading and Writing, 32*, 819–838. https://doi.org/ 10.1007/s11145-018-9886-x.

Tsuda, K., Muramatsu, N., Renandya, W. A., & Jacobs, G. M. (2023). Combining extensive reading while listening (ERWL) with cooperative learning. *JOALL (Journal of Applied Linguistics and Literature), 8*(1), 125–145. https://doi.org/10.33369/joall.v8i1.26128.

Tusmagambet, B. (2020). Effects of audiobooks on EFL Learners' reading development: Focus on fluency and motivation. *English Teaching, 75*(2), 41–67. https://doi.org/10.15858/engtea.75.2.202006.41.

Wang, S., & Kim, H. (2021). Extensive reading research in the EFL classroom of China: A qualitative meta-analysis. *Journal of Applied Linguistics, 44*(1), 111–125. https://doi.org/10.1515/CJAL-2021-0007.

Webb, S., & Chang, A. C. (2015). Second language vocabulary learning through extensive reading with audio support: How do frequency and distribution of occurrence affect learning? *Language Teaching Research, 19*(6), 667–686. https://doi.org/10.1177/1362168814559800.

Webb, S., Newton, J., & Chang, A. (2013). Incidental learning of collocation. *Language Learning, 63*(1), 91–120. https://doi.org/10.1111/j.1467-9922 .2012.00729.x.

Wilkins, A. J. (2019). Website XReading. *Reading in a Foreign Language, 31*(1), 140–146. http://hdl.handle.net/10125/66753.

Wisaijorn, P. (2017). Effects of extensive reading on Thai university students. *PASAA Paritat Journal, 32*, 29–61.

Yamashita, J. (2004). Reading attitudes in L1 and L2, and their influence on L2 extensive reading. *Reading in a Foreign Language, 16*(1), 1–19. http://hdl .handle.net/10125/66597.

Yamashita, J. (2013). Effects of extensive reading on reading attitudes in a foreign language. *Reading in a Foreign Language, 25*(2), 248–263. http:// hdl.handle.net/10125/66872.

Yip, P. C. (2000). *The Chinese lexicon: A comprehensive survey.* Routledge.

Zhou, J. (2017). Reading anxiety in learners of Chinese as a foreign language. *Reading in a Foreign Language, 29*(1), 155–173.

Zhou, J. (2018). *Component skills of reading among learners of Chinese as a second language* [Doctoral dissertation, University of Hawai'i at Manoa].

Zhou, J. (2021). The contribution of morphological awareness and vocabulary knowledge to Chinese as a second language reading comprehension: A path analysis. *Journal of Psycholinguistic Research, 51*, 55–74. https://doi.org/ 10.1007/s10936-021-09810-2.

Zhou, J. (2022). The effects of syntactic awareness to L2 Chinese passage-level reading comprehension. *Frontiers in Psychology, 12*, 783827. https://doi.org/ 10.3389/fpsyg.2021.783827.

Zhou, J. (2023). The contribution of radical knowledge and character recognition to L2 Chinese reading comprehension. *Journal of Psycholinguistic Research, 52*(2), 445–475. https://doi.org/10.1007/s10936-022-09880-w.

Zhou, J., & Day, R. R. (2021). Online extensive reading in EAP courses. *Reading in a Foreign Language, 33*(1), 103–125. http://hdl.handle.net/ 10125/67395.

Zhou, J., & Day, R. R. (2023). Establishing an extensive reading program in a Chinese as a foreign language context. *Reading in a Foreign Language, 35* (2), 222–246. https://hdl.handle.net/10125/67448.

Zhou, J., & Zhao, A. (2023). Review of Ponddy Reader. *Language Learning & Technology, 27*(1), 1–8. http://hdl.handle.net/10125/73513.

Zimmerman, B. J. (2008). Investigating self-regulation and motivation: Historical background, methodological developments, and future prospects. *American Educational Research Journal, 45*(1), 166–183. www.jstor.org/ stable/30069464.

Zulfariati, Z. (2023). Promoting EFL students' entrepreneurship enthusiasm: Using project-based learning in extensive reading activities. *ELP (Journal of English Language Pedagogy), 8*(1), 151–167. https://doi.org/10.36665/elp .v8i1.755.

Acknowledgments

This Element owes its existence to a number of excellent mentors who introduced me to ER and inspired me to continue ER research and practice. I would like to especially express my gratitude to Dr. Richard Day, "the founding father of ER," my PhD supervisor and a lifelong mentor. I would also like to acknowledge the Extensive Reading Foundation for its ongoing efforts to promote and publicize research on ER. This work has benefited greatly from the expertise of the series editors Jim McKinley and Heath Rose and two anonymous reviewers. I would also like to thank my students Mu Xueting, Liu Zhuoxin, Tang Zhiwei, Chen Rong, Zhu Xiaoyan, Chen Muhan, Shen Chenfei, and Yang Xinyu for their assistance. Lastly, I am grateful to my husband Chenghua Gao, my daughter Sarah, and my son Joe for inspiring me, and to my family members for their love and support.

Cambridge Elements ☰

Language Teaching

Heath Rose
University of Oxford

Heath Rose is Professor of Applied Linguistics at the University of Oxford and Deputy Director (People) of the Department of Education. Before moving into academia, Heath worked as a language teacher in Australia and Japan in both school and university contexts. He is author of numerous books, such as *Introducing Global Englishes, The Japanese Writing System, Data Collection Research Methods in Applied Linguistics,* and *Global Englishes for Language Teaching.*

Jim McKinley
University College London

Jim McKinley is Professor of Applied Linguistics at IOE Faculty of Education and Society, University College London. He has taught in higher education in the UK, Japan, Australia, and Uganda, as well as US schools. His research targets implications of globalization for L2 writing, language education, and higher education studies, particularly the teaching-research nexus and English medium instruction. Jim is co-author and co-editor of several books on research methods in applied linguistics. He is an Editor-in-Chief of the journal System.

Advisory Board
Gary Barkhuizen, *University of Auckland*
Marta Gonzalez-Lloret, *University of Hawaii*
Li Wei, *UCL Institute of Education*
Victoria Murphy, *University of Oxford*
Brian Paltridge, *University of Sydney*
Diane Pecorari, *Leeds University*
Christa Van der Walt, *Stellenbosch University*
Yongyan Zheng, *Fudan University*

About the Series
This Elements series aims to close the gap between researchers and practitioners by allying research with language teaching practices, in its exploration of research informed teaching, and teaching-informed research. The series builds upon a rich history of pedagogical research in its exploration of new insights within the field of language teaching.

Cambridge Elements $\equiv$

Language Teaching

Elements in the Series

Technology and Language Teaching
Ursula Stickler

Reflective Practice in Language Teaching
Thomas S. C. Farrell

English-Medium Instruction in Higher Education
David Lasagabaster

Task-Based Language Teaching
Daniel O. Jackson

Mediating Innovation through Language Teacher Education
Martin East

Teaching Young Multilingual Learners: Key Issues and New Insights
Luciana C. de Oliveira and Loren Jones

Teaching English as an International Language
Ali Fuad Selvi, Nicola Galloway and Heath Rose

Peer Assessment in Writing Instruction
Shulin Yu

Assessment for Language Teaching
Aek Phakiti and Constant Leung

Sociocultural Theory and Second Language Developmental Education
Matthew E. Poehner and James P. Lantolf

Language Learning beyond English: Learner Motivation in the Twenty-First Century
Ursula Lanvers

Extensive Reading
Jing Zhou

A full series listing is available at: www.cambridge.org/ELAT